THE ROYAL TEMPLE OF RAJARAJA

AN INSTRUMENT OF IMPERIAL COLA POWER

Dedicated to the memory of my grandfather
Justice R. Sankaranarayana Iyer

THE ROYAL TEMPLE OF RAJARAJA

AN INSTRUMENT OF IMPERIAL COLA POWER

GEETA VASUDEVAN

ABHINAV PUBLICATIONS

abhinav publications

First published in India 2003

Publishers
Shakti Malik
Abhinav Publications
E-37 Hauz Khas
New Delhi-110016 (INDIA)
Phones: 6566387, 6562784, 6524658
Fax: 91-11-6857009
e-mail: shakti@nde.vsnl.net.in

Website: http://www.abhinavexports.com

ISBN 81-7017-383-3

Phototypesetting and Processing by
Tara Chand Sons
Naraina, New Delhi

Printed at
D.K. Fine Art Press Pvt. Ltd.
Ashok Vihar, Delhi

CONTENTS

PREFACE

This book is based on my thesis entitled "ROYAL SHRINES AND THE GROWTH AND EXPANSION OF COLA POWER" for which I was awarded the Ph.D. degree by Madras University.

It is based on extensive research and indepth study of inscriptional data. A new interpretation to the temple as a Royal temple is attempted. The Royal Temple as an instrument and institution of imperial Cola power is illustrated through analytical and comparative study.

I am profoundly grateful to Dr. K.V. Raman (Prof. and Head of the Department of Ancient History and Archaeology, Madras University) for his valuable guidance and advice at every stage in my research.

I thank the authorities of the University of Madras and ICHR for permitting me to publish my thesis.

GEETA VASUDEVAN

1. The Rajarajesvaram (Brihadisvara Temple), Main Vimana.
Courtesy: Dr. K.V. Raman.

2. Rajaraja and Karur Devar (Brihadisvara Temple).
Courtesy: Dr. K.V. Raman.

3. Dance Sculpture (Brihadisvara Temple).
Courtesy: Dr. K.V. Raman.

4. Inscriptions (Brihadisvara Temple).
Courtesy: Dr. K.V. Raman.

10. Darasuram, Rajagambhira Mandapa, Chariot Shaped.
Courtesy: Dr. K.V. Raman.

9. Darasuram—Airavatesvara Temple, Main Vimana.
Courtesy: Dr. K.V. Raman.

12. Kailasanatha Temple—Kancipuram, Inner courtyard with Pallava lion pillars. Courtesy: Dr. K.V. Raman.

LIST OF ILLUSTRATIONS

COLOUR ILLUSTRATIONS

BLACK & WHITE ILLUSTRATIONS

METHOD OF TRANSLITERATION

Vowels	Tamil	Nagari	Consonants	Tamil	Nagari
a	அ	अ	k/g	க்	क / ग
ā	ஆ	आ	ṅ	ங்	ङ
i	இ	इ	c/ch	ச்	च/ज
ī	ஈ	ई	ñ	ஞ்	ञ
u	உ	उ	ṭ/ḍ	ட்	ट/ड
ū	ஊ	ऊ	ṇ	ண்	ण
e	எ	ए	t/d	த்	त/द
ē	ஏ	एए	n	ந்	न
ai	ஐ	ऐ	p	ப்	प
o	ஒ	ओ	m	ம்	म
ō	ஓ	ओओ	y	ய்	य
au	ஔ	औ	r	ர்	र
			l	ல்	ल
			v	வ்	व
			l̤	ழ்	
			ḷ	ள்	
			ṛ	ற்	
			n	ன்	
			ś		श
			ṣ		ष
			s		स
			ha		ह

For certain well-known and frequently occurring non-English terms we have indicated the diacritical marks at the first instance but have not continued them in the sequel deliberately to make it less cumbersome while reading in the typescript.

ABBREVIATIONS

Arch.	Archaeology
ARE	Annual Reports on Indian Epigraphy
ASI	Archaeological Survey of India
Ch.	Chapter
CVM	Caturvedimangalam
dist.	district
EC	Epigraphia Carnatica
Ed.	Editor or Edited
EI	Epigraphia Indica
esp.	especially
etc.	et cetera
GKC	Gangai Konda Cholapuram
Govt.	Government
IESHR	Indian Economic and Social History Review
IHC	Indian History Congress
insc.	inscription
JAS	Journal of Asian Studies
JESHO	Journal of the Economic and Social History of the Orient
JESI	Journal of the Epigraphical Society of India
JIH	Journal of Indian History
MVN	Muvendavelan
op. cit.	*opere citato*; in the work cited
Pub.	Published

Pud.	Pudukottai
QJMS	Quarterly Journal of the Mythic Society
Sec.	Section
SII	South Indian Inscriptions
SITI	South Indian Temple Inscriptions
TAS	Travancore Archaeological Series
Univ.	University
viz.	*videlicet*; namely
VN	Valanadu
Vol.	Volume

INTRODUCTION

Brahmanical Hinduism was the foremost religion of the people of South India in the middle of the first millennium A.D. It succeeded in uniting peoples of different regions and cultures; and the institution which helped in the propagation of this faith was the Hindu temple. The temple as a multi-faceted institution grew as a direct result of the *bhakti* movement. This movement, spearheaded by the *bhakti* saints—the *nāyanārs* and the *āḻvārs*, brought about a resurgence of temple-based Brahmanical Hinduism.

The Hindu temple as an institution was gaining importance even before the rise of the great Cola monarch, Rajaraja I. It was emerging as an institution which bound the community together socially, economically and through the medium of religion. Gradually the temple as the abode of the god and the palace as the abode of the king began to acquire certain common traits. These similarities grew over a period of time, as did the similarity between the temple paraphernalia and royal paraphernalia; and between the attendant or *parivāra* deities of the principal deity and the royal retinue of the monarch.

BHAKTI AND TEMPLE-BUILDING

The *bhakti* period started during the reign of the Pallavas. It was Appar, the *nāyanār* saint, who converted the great Pallava King Mahendravarman to the newly-resurrected Brahmanical religion. This period coincided with the withdrawal of royal patronage to non-Brahmanical religions like Jainism and Buddhism. The *bhakti* period saw the growth of innumerable temples to the principal gods, Siva and Visnu. Some temples already existed as small brick and mortar constructions. These insignificant little temples were eulogised by the saints in their hymns, the *Tēvaram* and the *Divyaprabandam.* Miracles were attributed to the presiding deities of these temples, and played no mean a role in spreading their fame far and wide. Thus, the hymns of the *bhakti* saints sanctified the temples and made them popular places of pilgrimage. The association of hundreds of temples with the *bhakti* saints in the Tamil country is mainly responsible for their continuing sanctity even 1500 years after they were built. In the minds of the Tamil people, the *nāyanārs* and the *āḻvars* continue to have a place as holy as the godhead about whom they sang.

Temple-building activities, thus, gained momentum in the beginning of Pallava rule. The Pallava kings became ardent temple-builders. It can be said that the Pallavas were the first to build *kaṟṟaḷis* or stone temples in the Tamil country. Mahendravarman and his son and successor, Narasimhavarman, experimented in carving temples in stone. Most of them were simple in plan and many of these temples were not consecrated by the saints. It is no surprise, then, that they lost their importance with the demise of their builders. Many undertakings like the five *rathas* of Mamallapuram remained incomplete. These as well as other temples were not of great importance for the common man, as they were not mentioned in the hymns of the *bhakti* saints. The Kailasanatha temple, one of the first grand stone temples built in the Tamil country, lost its glory soon after the eclipse of the Pallava dynasty. However, another grand Pallava royal temple at Kanci, the Vaikunta Perumal Temple, continues to this day as a holy shrine because it was visited by the saint Tirumaṅgai-Āḻvar. The Pallava period also saw the codification of the *āgamas*, or the rules that were to be followed in the construction of temples and in the conduct of worship in them. However, it was during the Cola rule that *āgama* worship became firmly established.

THE COLA PERIOD AND TAMIL CULTURE

The Cola empire under Rajaraja I and his successors extended over the entire Tamil country including Kerala, and established a pan-Tamil civilization over the conquered areas. The Cola empire extended over the whole of South India from coast to coast and in the north was bound by the river Tungabhadra and the Vengi frontier. (Vengi was almost an integral part of the empire between 1000 to 1150 A.D.) In the South, Cola hegemony extended over Sri Lanka too (though for a limited period). However, what is of note is that the Colas after Rajaraja established a uniform Tamil culture in all the regions under their control.

It was the first large empire to espouse the cause of Tamil as the official language. The *praśastis* of the Pallavas were generally in Sanskrit, the classical language of the North. In this and other respects, the Pallavas yearned to model themselves after the northern monarchs. Not only was Sanskrit the royal language, but the Pallavas performed *Vedic* sacrifices like the *rājasuya* very much like the North Indian kings. It was the Pallavas who introduced the practice of making land grants to families of Brāhmanas and settled them in exclusive Brāhmana hamlets called *brahmadēyas.* The Colas, too, made *brahmadēya* grants. In other respects, though, they did not imitate the northern kings and their *Vedic* practices. The Colas retained their Tamil identity while introducing Brahmanical rituals in temples. Even here, the emphasis is on rituals in temple worship and not so much on *Vedic* practices. They recognised the importance of the Brāhmana community as the cornerstone of organised Brahmanical religion, which they espoused wholeheartedly. However, they did not lose their identity as Tamil monarchs. It is significant that they were proud of their origins from the days of Karikala and traced their descent from the mythical Cola king in their *praśastis.* They also retained certain practices which were essentially of a Tamil or Dravidian character. For instance, some early Cola monarchs built *paḷḷipaḍais* for their dead ancestors. *Paḷḷipaḍais* were funerary monuments erected over dead kings, and such a custom was of ancient Tamil or Dravidian origin. The *liṅga* or deity was said to have been placed over the mortal remains of the dead king and regular worship was conducted. The Adityesvara at Tondamanad erected as a *paḷḷipaḍai* by Parantaka I to his father[1] and the Arinjigai-isvara at Melpadi built by Rajaraja I to commemorate Arinjaya are but two of the *paḷḷipaḍais* built by the Cola monarchs. By retaining their Tamil character, and by lending royal patronage to *āgamic* Saivism and Vaisnavism, as well as to the *Tēvaram* (hymns) and the *Divyaprabandam* they endeared themselves to their Tamil subjects. They encouraged both Sanskrit and Tamil learning.

The role played by the Colas in propagating temple worship was immense. They not only built several of their own, but also rebuilt existing temples in stone. Aditya I is credited with covering the banks of the Kaveri with a number of lofty and impregnable stone temples to Siva.[2] Parantaka I continued the work of his father; and the grand dowager of the Cola house, Sembiyam Madevi, built innumerable temples to Siva and Visnu and also rebuilt existing ones in stone.[3]

It was a time when religious sentiments reigned supreme. Bhakti Saivism was popularised by the Saiva *nāyanārs* and patronised by the 'imperial' Colas. The temple became the focus of the religious activities of the people. The religious feelings of the populace led to the increase in the financial resources of the temple. This additional wealth of the temples required an effective redistributive system. Gradually, the temple became a redistribution centre of wealth and services. The various social groups were directly or indirectly involved with the temple, either by way of extending their services to the temple, by helping in its administration or by carrying out the religious activities of the temple. In course of time, the entire community was interlocked through its association with the temple, and the temple became the nucleus of the religious, social and economic activities of the society.

THE TEMPLE AND POLITICAL POWER

The Cola kingdom, before Rajaraja, was confined to what was traditionally known as the Tamil country. Under Rajaraja, the great conqueror, vast regions belonging to the Kannada and Telugu country in the North, and Īlam in the South, came under the direct rule of the Cola monarchy. This large empire was controlled in various ways. Rajaraja stationed his army in strategic places to enforce Cola authority. (The mention of *paḍaividus* in several inscs., found in the regions annexed to the empire, gives evidence of this.[4]) The Colas also tried to superimpose a uniform administrative machinery over the local bodies in the conquered regions, as is seen from the insc.[5] belonging to Adi Rajendra in Polonnaruva in Īlam. However, these steps alone would have been insufficient in enforcing Cola authority effectively and permanently over the entire empire.

Herein, Rajaraja's eminence as a shrewd monarch can be seen. He utilised the institution of the Hindu temple to help establish and consolidate Cola hegemony over his vast empire. Up till now, the Hindu temple played the role of the nucleus of society by interacting with all peoples within the parameters of its influence—economically, socially and through the establishment of a spiritual bond. Rajaraja added an additional dimension to the Hindu temple by making it an instrument of political power and used it to establish and enhance Cola authority.

The temple as a focus of political power was, thus, the only next logical development. The focus of political and economic power shifted, even under the later Pallavas and the early Colas, from the *brahmadēya* to the temple. Power shifted to the temple administrative body which broke away from the control of local bodies. The newly-independent temple bodies transformed the temples into royal palaces for the deities. The paraphernalia of the medieval temple mirrored the royal court. For example, the temple idol's procession was similar to the king's procession. As already stated, Aditya I was credited with either renovating or building fresh temple complexes. It is quite likely that the Cola kings of the early period (traditionally dated between

5. Kiratarjuna Panel (Brihadisvara Temple). Courtesy: Dr. K.V. Raman.

6. Lakshmi (Brihadisvara Temple). Courtesy: Dr. K.V. Raman.

11. Kailasanatha Temple—Kancipuram, Sculptural Niches. Courtesy: Dr. K.V. Raman.

7. Gangaikondacolapuram, Main Vimana.
Courtesy: Dr. K.V. Raman.

8. Nataraja, Gangaikondacolapur
Courtesy: Dr. K.V. Rar

850-985 A.D.) built temples entirely out of their religious sentiments, in keeping with the surcharged *bhakti* atmosphere. Their attempts at temple-building might have been out of a desire to build permanent structures and to create a society of greater cohesion—a society that followed the Brahmanical order. The size of the temples was not considerable. Therefore, these early stone temples catered mostly to the religious needs of the people, which, in turn, bound the community together.

The Cola monarchs used this new institution to counteract the power wielded by local bodies, like the *sabhā* and the *ūr*. Vikrama Cola made several land endowments of entirely settled communities as tax-free (*iṛaiyili*) *dēvadāna* directly to the temple management staff, bypassing reference to local assemblies.[6] They not only patronised certain strategically located *brahmadēyas* and encouraged their separation from the *nāḍu* as *taniyūrs*, but focussed their attention on temples. Temple supervisory responsibility was increasingly withdrawn from local assemblies and administrative autonomy was bestowed upon full-time temple priests and employees. As pointed out by Kenneth Hall, "While previously temples were an extension of the community, in the later Cola period temples became the dominant fact in temple towns, such as Srirangam and Tanjavur as local residents came to serve the interest of these great temples."[7] This change seen as breaking the strength of previous ties between temples and the local elite further served the centralising ambitions of the Cola monarchs.

WHAT ARE BHAKTI TEMPLES?

There are two main arguments that this thesis attempts to examine. Firstly, it wishes to establish that there are two genres of temples—royal temples and non-royal temples. Non-royal temples can be *bhakti* temples or non-*bhakti* temples. Secondly, it attempts to show that the royal temple under Rajaraja I and his immediate successors was an institution used for the consolidation of Cola authority. These arguments have been put forth through the study of relevant, individual temples—both royal and non-royal. We shall attempt to explain what we mean by a *bhakti* temple.

The Saiva and Vaisnava saints sang the praises of the presiding deities of various holy shrines distributed in the Tamil country. Temples as places of worship became important as pilgrimage centres through this newly-acquired sanctity. In most cases these holy shrines were small temples in villages built of perishable material. The association of the saints with the shrines lent them an aura of sacredness. This, in turn, attracted the common man and royalty alike, who, spurred by religious feelings, donated liberally in cash and kind to the temples. Thus, the humble temples grew in size and importance.

Bhakti Saivism resulted (as already stated) in the increasing importance of the temple as an institution. The ideology of *bhakti* was responsible for the temple's role as the innovative focus through iconography, architecture, etc. These temples had their own mode of administration that usually involved the local assemblies and groups. That is to say, each temple grew from its roots in the locality of its origin. From humble beginnings, they increased in their size through local munificence. Right from the start, the temples were under the direct authority and control of the locality and its administration. Thus, the *sabhās* of *brahmadēyas* took decisions regarding the religious and economic affairs of the temples. The temples were, therefore, localised institutions. In times when the royal authority was restricted, the *sabhā* and *ūr* administration exercised authority unhindered over the temples under their control. At other times, when the royal authority was all-encompassing the government interfered in the administration of the temples. But this interference was generally limited to settling of disputes between the temple administration and the local bodies; enquiries into corruption and things of that kind, which could not be resolved by the local authorities between themselves. Thus, the royal government exercised its authority over these temples with the utmost discretion.

ROYAL PATRONAGE TO BHAKTI SHRINES

The holy shrines were sustained, not only by the donations of the lay devotees, but to a large extent through royal benefactions. Much of the expansion to the temple complexes could be accomplished through active participation of the kings and their retinue. As stated earlier, the kings of the Cola dynasty converted existing temples into permanent stone structures. Here, the king's role was that of a devotee (*bhakta*). At a time when kings were elevated through their acts of piety, it was a necessity for them to give benefactions to temples which had a hoary past of sanctity attached to them. In this way, they acquired merit in the eyes of their subjects and established their position as the foremost devotee of the lord. The kings were the ultimate donors. They took the lead in their ritual role as donors to Brāhmanas and temples alike. They actively participated in temple-building activities.

RITUAL KINGSHIP

Herein, the concept of 'ritual kingship' as mooted by Burton Stein can be seen.[8] Ritual, in South Indian history, played a predominant role in enhancing political authority and thereby promoted social relations. The *dēvadānas* and the *brahmadēyas* surrounding the temple complexes created a balanced social order, which was sought to be controlled by the Cola monarchs in their role as the ritual heads of society. The king was the greatest donor of grants, for it was the best manner in which he could get acceptance in the eyes of the people. The concept of kingship changed, according to Stein, from one based on royal sacrifice and genealogy—traced through royal *yajamanas* and fortified by military power to claim of authority based upon kingly maintenace of *dharma* and *dāna.* The Colas acquired from the Pallavas a conception of kingship which emphasised *dāna* as the dominant royal attributive. Brahmanical ritual kingship involved the transactional and redistributive process involving priests, kings, gods and ranked groupings.

The gradual changes that took place in the concept of kingship in South India can be understood from an analysis of Pallava kingship. In the earlier period, Pallava kings patronised and performed *Vedic* sacrifices. Later generations of the dynasty based their sovereignty on the sacrifices performed by their ancestors. For instance, the Uruvappali grant of Visnugopavaram[9] (late 5th c. A.D.) traces their ancestry and glory to the kings who had performed the horse sacrifice according to the proper rites. This format of beginning a grant with the glorification of the sacrifices was followed for almost two hundred years by the succeeding Pallava kings.

In course of time references to sacrifices receded in importance and divine genealogies became the base of sovereignty. The Pallava kings of the late 7th c. A.D. traced their descent from *Brahman, Brihaspati, Bhāradvāja, Drōna, Asvathāman,* to the eponymous Pallava and so on.[10]

The royal gifts or *dāna* was always important. It accompanied the sacrifices when kings gave *dakshina* and *dāna.* The granting of *brahmadēyas* was also an act of *dāna* and it became an occasion for the proclamation and expression of authority. Royal gifts were meaningful in terms of a conception of sovereignty. According to Nicholas Dirks, the gift itself became "an emanation of sovereignty, in which the endowed institution or individual(s) became actualized expressions of sovereignty."[11] Dirks goes on to expound that, as the endowed institutions, the temples were just as utilitarian as dams and canals, since they were just as necessary for prosperity. Vice-versa, dams and canals were as much places of ritual as temples since they were part of the social system of seeking welfare. That is why public works, irrigational projects etc., were usually connected with and administered under the auspices of temples in South India, from the Middle Pallava period through the Vijayanagara period. The temple, like the sacrifice, created prosperity. "The institutions that were spreading as a result of the royal *dānas* added to the depth and scale of the central polity. Temples were becoming increasingly important, both as institutions with constituencies and organizational capacities and as symbolic centres in which the growth of *pūjā* was responsible for transmitting new cultural and mythological formulations to larger and larger groups of people."[12]

The ideological framework of Cola ritual hegemony, says Stein, is analysable in terms of concrete institutions and the essentially administrative processes revolving around them. The keystone of the system of ritual hegemony was the royal Siva cult. Temples dedicated to Siva were the focal points in the network of Cola hegemony. The administration of ritual hegemony was centralized in the ruling government. From Rajaraja's time until the time of his successors in the 12th c., a deliberate effort was made to superimpose over South India a new modified ideological framework. "A royal cult of Siva (was) created in which the shrine of first the Tanjavur capital and later of GKC enjoyed special prominence and set the canonical style of temple worship for the entire macro region."[13]

The transformation of the king from one who was the guardian of the quarters to one in which he became identified with Visnu or Siva can be understood by studying the honours and rituals of temple worship. The marks of veneration conferred on the temple deities were, in many respects, similar to the honours shown to the sovereign. This concept is illustrated by the *paḻḻipaḍais* or funerary monuments built by the Cola monarchs. Grand Siva temples were erected over the remains of dead kings and services conducted in them. The identification of the Cola monarch (with Siva in this case) elevated the king to the realms of the gods.

Thus, by Rajaraja's time, the concept of the king as *dēvrāja* or god-king seems to have been well-developed. By building large temples to their chosen god and by giving liberally in cash and kind to temples (in fact lavishing much of the loot acquired in wars) the Cola kings of the middle period firmly established themselves as the ritual heads of society. The system of honours which involved the kings and their royal retinue and officers—with the king as the giver of honours—closely resembled the position of the principal deity and the subsidiary deities. The temple paraphernalia closely resembled the royal paraphernalia. The concept of ritual kingship was thus firmly established by the kings of the middle Cola period.

WHAT ARE ROYAL TEMPLES?

It was only in the second period of Cola rule—the reign of the great Rajaraja I and his equally illustrious son, Rajendra I—that the temple as an institution which wielded considerable economic and political power came into being. It was the great monarch Rajaraja I who perceived the limitless powers which could be exercised through a large-sized temple. Thus, he built one of the greatest edifices in the form of the Rajarajesvaram at Tanjavur, his capital city. The direct relation of patronage with the evolution of the Cola power structure and the royal city resulted in "an act of deliberate royal policy in creating a royal centre in imitation of the *bhakti* or sacred centre sung by the hymnists."[14] We, thus, see the temple's role in creating a ceremonial city, the symbol of centralising power. Therefore, all major temple projects were only for the royal centres.

The Rajarajesvaram or the Big Temple, as it is known popularly, was big not only in its size, but also in its reach. It is not the intention of this thesis to question the religious sentiments of Rajaraja and his unswerving faith in the Saiva religion. Granting that he built the Rajarajesvaram primarily for the glory of his chosen god, he also wished his temple to be the biggest one in the Tamil country, thus adding to his personal glory. Granting these motives which made him undertake such a mighty project, we should also attribute to him a keen sense of political expediency in building such a huge temple and endowing it with vast resources. It would be naive to state that Rajaraja built the temple purely for the religious merit of his family and people. It would be almost belittling his shrewd political sense if we do not recognise the fact that he realised the political and economic clout of a religious institution as large as this.

Thus, it would not be incorrect to state that in the second phase of Cola rule, the temple came into prominence as an institution which had considerable social, economic, religious and political power. This power was manipulated by the Cola kings who built temples of great sizes that became the foci of their empire. The kings, their royal retinue, the officers of the military and Cola administration gave liberally to these temples. In this way the Cola kings involved all their officers—civil and military—actively in the affairs of their temples. The administration created for these temples of such immense size and wealth was controlled directly by the royal government. Lands were granted to them not only in the core area of Tanjavur and its environs, but also in far-off places like Tondaimandalam and Īlam. The clause in religious donations—which states that a grant made to a temple cannot be revoked by anyone—was used to ensure that the lands granted in these far-off places would continue to be associated with the temple, even if they were no longer under the direct suzerainty of the Colas. (It was another matter that several grants of their predecessors were revoked by the kings themselves.) By granting lands in areas which were not directly under the Cola authority, they brought about a religious bond between the temple (under the direct control of the government) and the people of these regions. Through this bond was ensured the economic link between the two and thus the political control over these areas—albeit indirectly.

Another important motive in constructing a mighty temple for Siva in his capital city and endowing it with enormous wealth and other resouces was to manifest royal backing to Saivism. As pointed out by Raman[15] during the Pallava period, the royal ventures were not one-sided. Both the Saiva and Vaisnava temples received more or less equal support. But from the Colas of the Vijayalaya line, we see the sectarian polarisation taking a sharper edge. They bestowed greater attention on Siva temples—the efforts of Sembiyam Madevi, Aditya I and Parantaka I are well-known. The four major temple ventures of the Cola period—the Rajarajesvaram at Tanjavur by Rajaraja I, the Gangaikondacolisvarar by Rajendra I, the Airavatesvar at Darasuram by Rajaraja II and the Kampaharesvarar at Tribhuvanam by Kulottunga III—were all for Siva. The motive was clear—glorifying Saivism in preference to Vaisnavism and other religions. The sculptural themes in these temples clearly furnished supporting evidence for this. Sculptures like Lingodbhava, Śarabhamurthi, etc., which are highlighted in these temples show the superiority of Saivism over Vaisnavism. From the perspective of the evolution of religion in the Tamil country, it cannot be gainsaid that a primary motive for constructing the mighty temples and lavishly furnishing them as the focus centre of religious and cultural gatherings and activity was to popularise Saivism with massive royal support.

As stated before, the royal control over the *bhakti* shrines was superficial in the earlier period. It acted mostly as a benevolent superintendent who exercised his powers only in times of crisis, and then too, only with the consultation of the local groups, *nāṭṭār* and *ūrār*. The *dēvadānas* and the *brahmadēyas* surrounding the local temples enjoyed much autonomy. This anomaly was set right by the Cola kings of the middle period when they started building temples of their own. Taking full advantage of the enormous possibilities afforded for enlarging their political hold over their vast territories, by appealing to the religious fervour of the people, they—Rajaraja I and his successors—built temples of enormous proportions. They created large *dēvadāna* lands through land grants and administered them directly by creating a vast, complicated redistributive network, whereby material and personnel were transferred and brought under the direct control of the royal government. The remuneration for the temple functionaries, thus transferred, may have been attractive and they seem to have been well looked after through the grant of house plots, land grants, etc.

Whether the remuneration was as good as that which they would have got in the temples from where they were transferred, is not clear; because with the demise of their patrons, the size of the temple family seems to dwindle; this despite the fact that here they were assured of a steady income. One explanation for this phenomenon seems to be the policy of the monarchs themselves. Rajaraja took much pains to bring people from other temples of his kingdom to his own temple at Tanjavur. His son, Rajendra, undid the work of his father. When he built his own big temple at Gangaikondacolapuram, his new capital, he did not take pains to find his own temple functionaries; instead he seems to have transferred *en masse* most of the secular functionaries from his father's temple and appointed them to his temple. He even regranted some of the *dēvadāna* lands belonging to the Rajarajesvaram to his temple. However, even his own great monumental achievement was short-lived.

DIFFERENCES

Herein lies the crucial difference between a royal temple and a *bhakti* temple. A *bhakti* temple started as a small structure and grew from its roots, as it were, indigenously. It grew in size and importance due to the patronage of the laity and royalty, as a result of the sanctity bestowed on it by its association with the venerable saints. The royal temple, on the other hand, was a sudden development, built and nurtured almost entirely by the kings and their entourage. One cannot trace the growth of royal temples in the same way as one can the growth of *bhakti* temples. It was consecrated as a complete institution.

A royal temple was built by a monarch usually in the capital city with the express desire of sanctifying it. The temple as the pivot of society was fully realised and appreciated by the Middle Colas. By building cities with big temples as their centres, the Colas attempted at creating the prerequisite conditions of an important urban centre. However, the royal cities built by them lacked the sanctity that the cities with *bhakti* or holy shrines as their nuclei had. Therefore the royal builders had them sanctified by getting hymns composed in their praise by the spiritual preceptors. Despite this, the glory of these temples was often short-lived. The glory of the great Kailasanatha Temple at Kanci, the Rajarajesvaram at Tanjavur and many other great Cola royal temples faded away with the death of their creators. The elaborate administrative set-up and economic arrangements of these temples were almost disbanded or reduced in size. It is a curious point that most of these temples remained incomplete. On the other hand, the *bhakti* temples were sanctified by their association with the hymnists, and they did not require a powerful king's munificence to sustain them. They survived and grew due to the religious fervour and patronage of the common man.

PERIOD UNDER STUDY

Temple-building activities reached their zenith during the middle Cola period—popularly dated from the reign of Rajaraja I to the beginning of the reign of Kulottunga I (985-1070). The royal temple as the expression of royal power reached its maturity in the two great Cola temples of this period—the Rajarajesvaram of Rajaraja at Tanjavur and the Gangaikondacolisvaram of Rajendra at Gangaikondacolapuram. This study restricts itself to this particular period for several reasons.

Vast empire: Rajaraja expanded the Cola kingdom and gave it the dimensions of an empire. Large areas from the R. Tungabhadra to Northern Sri Lanka and the entire Tamil region, including Kerala, were part of this empire. From an ordinary Maharaja, the Cola monarch acquired the status of a *Chakravartin*. Rajendra added to the conquests of his father by undertaking a grand *digvijaya*, in the course of which he is said to have gone to the banks of the R. Ganga and brought home its waters. Kalinga and other kingdoms became subordinate states, accepting the suzerainty of the Cola monarch.

Therefore, it was during the middle period that the size of the empire was at its greatest. From the reign of Kulottunga I in 1070 A.D., the borders of the empire contracted to the confines of the three traditional Tamil kingdoms plus the kingdom of Vengi. After that, the Cola empire never reached such dimensions as it did in the middle period. Thus, this period which saw the expansion of the empire to its maximum size, coincided with the peak of Cola power. Cola hegemony was established through various institutions, like the army, governmental institutions and (for the first time) through the medium of the royal temple. Therefore, no other period would justify such a study.

Administrative set-up: Needless to say, this period saw the Cola administrative acumen at its best. The extent of the empire necessitated a tight and effective administrative set-up. The empire was divided into a number of divisions and subdivisions based on geographical considerations. Each major division (or *maṅḍalam*) was under a Cola governor (quite often a royal prince). The governors were assisted by a hierarchical bureaucracy and army officers. The bureaucracy was divided into a higher and lower cadre. They were called *perundanam* and *śirudanam* respectively. The empire was governed by a well-honed administration. It is, therefore, not surprising that large institutions like the royal temples would have had administrative bodies capable of handling vast resources, both in men and wealth. A study of the administration of the Rajarajesvaram reveals the astute administrative capabilities of the Colas of the middle period.

The large number of Cola officers like *mūvēndavelārs, pallavaraiyārs, brahmamārāyans, ōlaināyagans,* etc. constituted the Cola bureaucracy which directly administered the empire. Revenue officers like the *puravuvari* kept in contact with local bodies. The lands were systematically surveyed and taxation levied on the basis of fertility and yield. The inscs. reveal the functioning of a network of revenue officials to assess and collect taxes on lands, water-supply, tolls and custom duties. Thus, the Cola bureaucracy administered the empire effectively as a cohesive whole.

Core region: The region known popularly as Colamandalam remained the core region until 1250 A.D. This was the region directly under governmental control even during the reign of the weaker monarchs. Most of the records analysed for this study belong to this region. They show how the royal power emanated from the core region of Colamandalam. Needless to say, royal institutions like the royal temple effectively knit together the *nāḍus* and the *vaḷanāḍus* of Colamandalam.

Peripheral areas: States like Īlam, Kalinga, Vengi and the Kannada regions constituted the periphery of the empire. These regions were the first to break away and assert their independence whenever the centre was weak, or when the Cola king's attention was diverted in wars of aggression. These peripheral regions came under the Cola control in the Middle Cola period. Under strong kings like Rajaraja I and Rajendra I, these areas submitted to the control and authority of the Cola government, though they tried to retain their distinct identity. It is to the credit of the Cola monarchs that they did not seek to destroy this identity, but only superimposed their authority on them. That is why revenue systems and local administration were not interfered with in the conquered territories like Īlam. It is in these areas that the importance and relevance of the royal temple is seen. By linking the conquered territories with the institution of the royal temple, Rajaraja realised the importance of the religious medium. Even the efficient Cola bureaucracy would have been wanting in controlling areas as distant as these. Rajaraja understood the need for an institution like the royal temple to assist in the control and administration of these areas, which were far away from the core region. Thus, the importance of royal temples increased in the light of extending Cola hegemony over the conquered regions through the medium of religion.

Āgamic expansion: Temple worship according to *āgamic* rules can be said to have started in the Pallava times. However, *āgamic* worship became fully established in the period under study. The temple complex was expanding, with niches for various deities on stipulated sides of the walls of the sanctum *Linga* worship in Siva temples was universalised. Additional *prākāras* were being added and subsidiary shrines came up in these *prākāras.* The *āgamic* rules for sculpture, architecture, rituals, etc. were being strictly followed in temples of this period. The *āgamic* expansion of rituals led to the need for various kinds of temple functionaries. The temple *parivāra* expanded considerably. Therefore, this is the crucial period which affords the necessary backdrop against which the royal temple as an institution attained full maturity. It was also a period of institutionalisation of Saiva canons and hymns. Rajaraja is credited with having recovered the missing *Tēvaram* hymns and made grants for their singing in the Tanjavur temple. He also deified the Tamil saints and instituted festivals in their honour.

SCOPE OF STUDY

Much research has been done in studying temples of various periods—either as individual case studies or as a collective group. These studies have thrown light on certain interesting and valuable data regarding the art and architecture of temples belonging to different periods. Some studies have helped to trace the development of religion and religious practices. Valuable work has been done on the organisational aspect of temples—their administration, finances, etc. Studies on individual temples have been useful as reference material. Mention may be made of such temple-based studies of individual temples as K.K. Pillay's *Suchindram Temple,* K.V. Raman's *Sri Varadarajaswami Temple—Kanci,* B. Venkatraman's *Rajarajesvaram—The Pinnacle of Cola Art*—only to mention a few. These studies have made an indepth study of these important individual temples—from tracing their history to analysing their art and architecture and their administration through the ages. These works have been invaluable as guidelines for several research theses by providing the format to be followed by future scholars. Added to these are S.R. Balasubramaniam's monumental works on Cola art, *Early Cola Temples, Middle Cola Temples,* etc., which have studied groups of temples belonging to different periods. Papers have also been written on other aspects of temples. Scholars have analysed temple administration, the growth and role of the *maṭhas,* the growth of Saivism and Vaisnavism and other cults and practices.

However, in all these studies the temple has been taken as a homogeneous unit. Though mention has been made of the role played by kings belonging to various dynasties, no conscious attempt has been made to differentiate between a royal temple and a *bhakti* or non-royal temple. As has been delineated earlier, the two were quite different in origin and composition. One had its humble origin and grew through the ages by the contributions of many generations. The additions and changes made by different dynasties to the original complex can be traced; the gradual growth in the size of its *parivāra* can be studied; and the growth of the temple complex as a whole can be understood. In short, non-royal or *bhakti* temples provide ample material for independent studies of a historical nature.

In contrast the royal temple, as has been shown, was a sudden development. It was a fully-developed institution as visualised by its builder, and had its entire complex built during his lifetime (barring a few minor additions). The temple functionaries were appointed by and responsible to the royal government—unlike the non-royal temple, where the administration was initially in the hands of local bodies and later in the hands of independent temple managing bodies.

In most aspects, the two types of temples differed greatly. Therefore, 'Temple Studies' as such cannot be a homogeneous study. Temples have to be differentiated as 'royal temples' and '*bhakti* or non-royal temples'. Only then can we analyse the rationale behind the growth and development (or the lack of it) of individual temples. Only by recognising the differences in their character, can we appreciate the motivation behind building large-sized temples by the Cola monarchs. We have to recognise this basic difference between the two types of temples—the *bhakti* temples which came up and were nourished through the religious fervour of the people, both laymen and kings, and royal temples which were built by their royal builders not only as an act of piety but for reasons other than purely religious. Royal temples were a manifestation of the greatness of kings (as envisaged by themselves). They were built to enhance the kings in the eyes of their subjects as the foremost *bhaktas* and to propagate their chosen god. They had political dimensions. The royal temples, as has been seen, were used as instruments of royal power to control the empire in all ways. Thus, the royal temples, as visualised by the middle Colas, were a distinct class and as such have to be analysed and studied in a different light.

It is with this realisation (of the distinctive character of the royal temple) that this thesis seeks to analyse the composition and character of royal temples of the middle Cola period. It goes on to analyse the role of royal temples in the spread of Cola power and hegemony. Thus, the study is confined to the period of maximum power wielded by the Cola kings—the period of Rajaraja I and his successors. The study seeks to examine the role of the royal temple as an instrument of Cola power.

METHODOLOGY

The methodology adopted involves an indepth analysis of the inscriptions of the various temples taken up for study. The temple of the Rajarajesvaram provides copious epigraphical material belonging to Rajaraja's period. These inscriptions have been valuable for scholars analysing Cola administration, as the walls are a veritable registry of all the transactions in cash and men involving the temple. These inscriptions have therefore been extensively studied, though they have not been exhaustively interpreted. Thus, B. Venkatraman's work uses the inscriptions to analyse the administrative set-up, the economic wealth, the art and architecture, etc. of this celebrated temple. The detailed administrative descriptions have been used by Stein and others to describe temple administration in general.

In this thesis, an attempt would be made to reinterpret existing data to substantiate the arguments put forth and to present an integrated picture of the Rajarajesvaram as a royal temple. It would involve, firstly, the use of relevant inscriptions. Thus, inscriptions dealing with the economic/social/religious and political matters are analysed in detail. Secondly, the emphasis is not in studying the temple per se, but in analysing the role played by the royal temple in enhancing the growth and consolidation of Cola power, and to establish the argument that the royal temple was an important arm of the government. The focus would therefore be on the builder and his possible motives.

While the main thrust of the thesis is the study of Cola temples, one or more major *bhakti* or non-royal temples have been analysed for a comparative study. This would help in highlighting the basic differences between *bhakti* temples, on the one hand, and royal temples on the other and help to establish the distinct character of the royal temples. Though the period of study chosen is the middle Cola period—this being the mature period in the development of the royal temple as an institution—a royal temple belonging to the pre-Cola period has been analysed. This would help to understand the development of the royal temple as an institution. Apart from inscriptions, iconographical themes have been analysed to highlight some of the arguments put forth in this thesis.

REFERENCES

1. 230 of 1903.
2. Anbil Plates.
3. ARE 1926, II, 22.
4. EI, XVIII, 38.
5. SII, IV, 1392.
6. 272, 273, 275, 276, 301 of 1907.
7. Kenneth R. Hall, "Peasant State & Society in Cola Times...", IESHR, Vol. XVIII, 81, No. 3 & 4.
8. Burton Stein, All the Kings' Mana, p. 29ff.
9. Indian Antiquary, Feb. 1876, p. 50ff.
10. Kuram Plates, SII, I, p. 144ff & Vayalur Plates, EI, XVIII, p. 145ff.
11. Nicholas B. Dirks, "Political Authority & Structural Change in Early South Indian History", IESHR.
12. Ibid.
13. Stein, Peasant State..., p. 357.
14. Champakalakshmi, R., "Urbanisation...", IHC, 1986, p. 34ff.
15. Raman, K.V., "Vaishnavism Under Rajaraja I", Seminar on Rajaraja I.

Chapter I

THE TEMPLE IN PRE-RAJARAJA PERIOD—A BACKGROUND STUDY

THE KAILASANATHA TEMPLE—KANCI A ROYAL SHRINE OF THE PALLAVAS

From the 7th c. till the 9th c. A.D., the Pallavas were the most powerful monarchs of South India, and under them the Dravidian style of temple architecture could be said to have taken final shape. The transition to the structural temple can be traced starting with the cut-in cave temples of Mahendravarman, through the beautiful monolithic temples of his son and successor, Narasimhavarman at Mamallapuram. They were the first kings of the Tamil country to build structural temples in stone, and the credit for this goes to the great temple-builder of the Pallavas—Rajasimha. Among his many significant temples is the Kailasanatha temple or the Rajasimhēśvara at Kanci, the capital city of the Pallavas. This temple was completed by his son, Mahendravarman and his queen, Rangapataka. With a total height of 66.33 ft (20.27 m) it was the tallest structure of its time and even now its *vimāna* ranks among the tallest temple *vimānas* in the South.

After the construction of the Shore Temple at Mamallapuram (which he named the Kshatriyasimhesvara), the Kailasanatha Temple was the major temple constructed by Rajasimha. In its size and conceptualisation, it surpassed any other structure of the time. Therefore, we can say that the Kailasanatha temple was the first major attempt by a Tamil monarch to design and create a temple complex of large proportions, with *gōpura* entrance, side cloisters, tall central *vimāna* and several subsidiary cells to accommodate a vast assemblage of divinities.

It will be interesting to see how the royal temple was viewed and conceived by the Pallavas. We can take the Pallavas as a case study because they preceded the Colas in building royal temples, especially in their capital cities. The Kailasanatha temple or the Rajasimhēśvara was very much a royal temple. In fact, it was the Pallavas who started the trend of naming their patron deity after themselves. Thus, the Rajasimhēśvara was the Siva temple named after its builder, Rajasimha. This trend was followed by the early Colas, for example Vijayalaya-Colīśvara, Adityēśvara, and in later times, the Rajarajēśvaram.

All the Pallava inscs. in this temple give the 'titles' of the king and his son. The administrative details are gleaned from the inscs. belonging to the Cola and the Vijayanagara periods. The early Cola inscs. belong to Parantaka I and continue upto the period of Rajadhiraja. However, the service in the temple was stopped in the reign of Kulottunga I; the temple was closed; and the temple land and compound were sold (according to a record belonging to the Vijayanagara period).[1] Thus, for quite some time the temple was closed for worship. This record supports our arguments that the life of a royal temple was short (usually only till the lifetime of its builder or his immediate successors).

The Kailasanatha temple had no pretensions to sanctity. It had no associations with the *bhakti* saints or with any significant religious event. This drawback was sought to be rectified by the Middle Cola rulers like Rajaraja I and Rajendra I, who also built royal temples but had them sanctified by having sacred hymns composed on them and including them in the *Tiruviśaippa*, the Saiva Canon.

Thus the Pallava temple of Rajasimhesvara is an interesting example for studying the contrast between the differing conceptions and executions of the royal temple as an institution by the Pallavas, who were the pioneers in the field of building grand, royal, structural temples; and their successors, the Colas, who improved upon the idea of the Pallavas and converted an architectural monument and a religious institution into an instrument of the royal government wielding considerable influence. In fact, it can be said that the Colas improved upon the Pallava style of temple-building. Further, the Colas viewed the temple not just as a beautiful architectural edifice and a symbol of kingship, but as an institution which closely interacted with the surrounding areas and the prevailing religious atmosphere.

LAND GRANTS

The Kailasanatha Temple was built in the town of Tirukaṟṟalippuram which belonged to the Kaliyūr-Kōṭṭam of Tondainadu. Kaliyūr-Kōṭṭam comprised portions of Chingelput and North Arcot dists.

There are seven inscs. in this temple belonging to the Pallavas,[2] all of which give the *birudas* of the King Rajasimha and his son, Mahendravarman. The genealogy of the Pallavas starting with their mythical ancestors, their war exploits, etc. are mentioned too. But not much is said about the administrative arrangements of the temple, the endowments made and other details regarding its management.

Almost all the early Pallava grants were copper-plate charters. The inscs. on the walls of the Vaikunṭaperumaḷ temple at Uttaramerur, which mention grants by individuals and others were later in date belonging to the second period of Pallava rule (i.e. after Nandivarman Pallava Malla). That endowments were made to royal temples by their builders and successors is evident from the Kuram CP charters, belonging to the period of Paramesvara Varman I.[3] This charter states that the Siva temple called Vidyavinita-Pallava-Paramesvara, which was built by Vidyavinita-Pallava (a relative of the king), was situated in the village of Kuram near Kanci. This Vidyavinita-Pallava bought 1200 *kuḻis* of land (from the villagers) for which he paid in gold. Land was purchased to burn tiles for building a temple, to dig a tank and to build houses and house-gardens to be allotted to those who had to perform worship in the temple. The remaining land was cultivated for providing the customary offerings. Paramesvaravarman I gave the village of Paramesvaramangalam to this temple as *arcanābhoga*, for making repairs to the temple, and also as *brahmadēya* to twenty *caturvedins*. Similarly, the Muktesvara Temple at Kanci, built by Queen Dharmamahadevi,[4] had a temple establishment comprising of 54 temple functionaries. The revenue of a whole village was made over to the temple. According to the Velurpalaiyam Plates, the king granted the village for maintaining the services (*pūjāśatrādikarmane*) in the temple of God Mahadeva at Srikallupalli.

A record from the Kailasanatha Temple belonging to the 3rd year of Ko-Rajakesarivarman[5] mentions the town of Tirukarralippuram (the town of the holy stone temple). In the Pallava times, the Kailasanatha Temple was known as the Rajasimhesvara, or simply as Tirukaṟṟaḷi (the sacred stone temple). The latter must have been the common man's reference to the royal temple; it shows that a stone temple was not a common sight. Kancipuram is mentioned separately from Tirukarralippuram; therefore, this could refer to the town/village which was granted to the royal temple as *dēvadāna* by its builder. Tirukarralippuram means the settlement or village of the temple. It was evidently a new settlement established by Rajasimha with his temple as the nucleus in a suburb of the city of Kanci. There is no reference to this place prior to Rajasimha. This village must have been granted to maintain services and rituals in the temple, as well as to provide remuneration for the functionaries of the temple.

From an insc.[6] belonging to a late period, we come to know that the Kailasanatha temple was endowed with the revenue from a village. An insc.[7] belonging to the 34th year of Kulottunga I states that a royal grant of 2 *vēlis* of land south of Kanci was made to the Siva temple of Anēkatangapadam in Kanci. These lands were close to the Kailasanatha Temple. It is to be noted that these formed a part of those gifts of Kulottunga I which were declared unlawful and restored to the Kailasanatha temple in the time of Kampana-udaiyar, who was the general of the Vijayanagara army and was responsible for extending the Vijayanagara kingdom to the Tamil country. This record[8] is dated Śaka 1286 (1364 A.D.). His officer, Koppanagal, addressed a royal order to the authorities of the Rajasimhesvara-udaiyar, at Kanci. It states that in the time of Kulottunga Choladeva the temple was closed, its land (*tirunāmattu-kāṇi*) sold and the temple compound (*tiruviruppu*) and the environs of the temple (*tirumaḍaivilagam*) were given over to the temple close to the royal temple. Thus, the temple seems to have been endowed with land for maintaining the services and for remunerating the temple staff. The insc. goes on to say that the amount, which had been cancelled and given away according to the writing on the stone (formerly engraved), shall be managed and attended to without fail.

A damaged insc.[9] of Rajendra I in the Kailasanatha Temple refers to a grant of paddy, gold and cash. The next land grant belongs to the Vijayanagara dynasty, and is dated Śaka 1286.[10] This royal order of Kampana-udaiyar granted the whole village of Murungai in Panmanadu, a division of Manavirkottam, as *sarvamānya*, free from taxes (*iraiyiḷi*). A whole *sannidhi* street belonged to this temple as *sarvamānya.* Another royal order[11] of the same king conveyed by his officer gave some land as *kāṇi* to the *maṭha* near the temple.

MONEY-LENDING ACTIVITIES

The details concerning the economic activities of the temple are available only in the records belonging to the post-Pallava period. The cash endowed to the temple was lent out on interest to various groups, and the interest on it was paid into the temple treasury in the form of ghee or oil for lamps, or in the form of paddy for offerings. In the third year of Ko-Rajakesarivarman, the temple treasury invested with the villagers of Menalur 18 *kalañju*, 3 *manjāḍi* and 1 *kunṛi* gold. The villagers pledged themselves to supply daily 1 *ulakku* oil for one perpetual lamp, as interest on the sum they received.

In the 4th year of Ko-Rajakesarivarman,[12] the villagers of Kalladuppur received from Candesvara at Tiruvottur (a division of this *kōṭṭam*) 8... of gold, i.e. 20 *kalañju* gold. The *mahāsabhā* of Kalladuppur (in Virappedunadu of Kaliyurkottam) undertook to supply 90 *nalis* of paddy yearly to feed *Sivabrahmanas.*

Three records of Rajaraja I[13] mention cash transactions between the temple treasurers (*Śiva-panḍārigaḷ*) and the people of different villages (all belonging to Kaliyurkottam). The first record belonging to his 12th year states that the interest was in the form of yearly supply of paddy. In case of default on interest, the *sabhā* agreed to pay a fine of *pon* daily. In the second record (3rd year of Rajaraja), the interest was 1 *uḻakku* oil daily on an investment of 15 *kalañju* gold. The third record also mentions the investment for an identical supply. It states that 1 *uḻakku* oil daily amounted to 7 *nāḻis* and 1 *uri* per month. (The measure of *nāḻi* was equal to 1 Rajakesari—a royal measure.) The stipulated quantity of oil or ghee was handed over to those in charge of the measure (*nāḻigai*) in the temple. They were called *naligaiudaiyargal.*

CATTLE GRANTS

Two grants[14] belonging to the 15th year of Parantaka I mention grants of sheep for lamps by an individual called Candraparakrama-vira. The first grant was for 270 sheep for maintaining three lamps. These cattle were handed over to a shepherd called Candraparakrama-*manṛāḍi* (different from the donor). He agreed to supply on a permanent basis 3 *uḻakku* ghee daily to the *nāḻigaiudaiyārgaḻ* or else pay a fine of one *mañjāḍi* of gold every day. In the second grant, the same donor gave 180 sheep for 2 lamps or *nandaviḷakku,* to be handed over to Kalakopa-vira-*manṛāḍi,* who pledged to implement the endowment or else pay a fine of 1 *kunṛi* gold daily. An insc. of the 26th year of

Tribhuvanacakravarti Rajarajadeva states that an individual agreed to supply on a daily basis one *uḷakku* ghee for 5 *sandhi viḷakku* (twilight) lamps.

ADMINISTRATION

The Pallava inscs. do not give any information on the administrative set-up of the Kailasanatha temple. They are only laudatory verses of the Pallava royal builder and his son. Therefore, we have to look elsewhere for references to the administration of the temples in Pallava times.

A 16th year insc.[15] of Nripatungavarman refers to the *gaṇapperumakkaḷ* of the temple of Sailesvaram in Paramesvaramangalam, who received an interest of 11 *kalañju* gold from an individual and agreed to provide offerings for midday services. The temple administrative body was also called *taḷipparivāram.* Twelve superintendents in the temple establishment can be seen in the statement, *"adhyakśadvādaśa-dēvakarmi-bhyah".*[16] The number 12 seems to have been a model one in Pallava times.

The land grants for the Kuram temple were divided into 25 parts.[17] Three parts were to be enjoyed by two *Brāhmanas*, who performed the divine rites in the temple and looked after the repairs of the temple. One part was set aside for reciting the Bharata in the *mandapa.* When the Pallava Vidyavinita built the Siva temple at Kuram, he bought 1200 *kuḷis* of land to build the temple, tank, etc.; houses and house-gardens for those who had to perform the worship in the temple. It also states that one *Bappabhaṭṭāraka* (a *yagña bhattar*) was made responsible for protecting the gifts set apart for the performance of the sacred rites in the temple. This person was either the *guru* of Nandivarman III or a *dēvakarmi*—executive officer who was a member of the superintending committee of the temple.

Tānattārs: When the Kailasanatha temple was built, and as long it was the royal temple of the Pallavas, it was likely that no trustees would have been appointed from outside. The reference to *tānattārs* is a late one. In the Pallava period this prestigious temple would have been administered directly by the royal government. The paucity of any administrative details in the temple makes it difficult for us to identify the status of the managing committee. The reference to the trustees is found in a Vijayanagara royal order and is addressed to the authorities of the temple.[18] The *dēvakarmis* (the executive officers) and the accountant or the *kaṇakku* were signatories to any temple document; local headmen like Uttaramerur-udaiyan and other local dignitaries also acted as trustees. Although this is a very late record, there are references to *tānattārs* even during Pallava times. A record from the Muktesvara temple in Kanci,[19] built by Queen Dharmamahadevi, also mentions managers of the temple. The term used is *taliāḷvar* and it probably refers to the three Brāhmana *pūjāris*.

Treasurer: The treasurers were known as *Śivapaṇḍārigal*. The *banḍāram* or the *banḍāri* was the treasurer and was in charge of the storehouse. They were in charge of the rations of paddy, ghee and other items paid in kind into the treasury of the temple. The *poṇ-banḍāram* was the gold treasury. There are several references to the stipulated quantity of ghee being handed over to those in charge of the temple measure. These people were known as *nāḻigaiuḍaiṇārgaḷ*. Similarly, there are references to villagers receiving cash from the *banḍāram* for which they had to pay interest in the form of ghee or paddy.

OTHER FUNCTIONARIES

Dancing Girls: Dancers were attached to temples—whether *bhakti* or royal. Though there is no mention of them in the inscs. of this temple, we get references from other temples of the Pallava period. The Muktesvara temple of Kanci mentions as many as 42 dancers.

Drummers and Musicians: They have been a part of the retinue of all temples. The sculptures of temples, like the Vaikuntaperumal of Kanci, show musicians playing on the drums and the lute. They were paid in paddy and were intimately connected with the services in the temples.

Archakas: They were the priests who did the actual *pūjā* in the sanctum. Generally, they were a part of the body of trustees and were given *kāṇi* known as *archanābhōga*.

Mahēśvaras: Along with the *pūjāris*, they ensured that the services were conducted in accordance with the *āgamas*. Among the titles of Rajasimha was the title of *āgamapriyah*. The Pallavas were among the earliest monarchs to ensure that temple services were conducted according to the *āgamas*. The royal order of Koppangal,[20] addressed to the *tānattārs*, gave the *maṭha*, near the temple, some land as *kāṇi* to a certain Gangayar of Tirumudukunram. This Gangayar (*Perumān*) was the teacher of one of the *Mahēśvaras* of Tirumudukunram. The order was signed, among others, by the *mahēśvaras* and *tānattārs*.

Temple Nivendakaras: There are references from other temples[21] of male temple servants appointed to clean the temple premises. They were called *viḷakkum tavaśigaḷ*. They would have been given a daily share of the food. If the *taḷipparivāram* of the Muktesvara temple totalled 54, then that of the Kailasanatha temple must have been much bigger.

TERRITORIAL REACH

From a study of the inscs. recording land grants, as well as cash investments and endowments of sheep for lamps, we can see that almost all the mentioned villages or areas were in and around the temple town of Tirukarralipuram. Therefore, the area of influence of this royal temple of the Pallavas was limited. Even during the reign of the Pallavas, who prided themselves in having built such a grand stone temple, the village or the lands close to the temple seem to have been granted as *dēvadāna*. This was done mainly to ensure that the daily services were conducted properly and that the temple functionaries were well-paid.

PATRONAGE

As stated above, the Pallavas used their royal temple to record their *praśastis* and their *biruḍas*. No doubt, they would have taken care to endow their royal undertaking substantially. Special grants were made for festival feeding, for *Siva Brahmanas* and others. Similarly, separate grants were made for the establishment of *mathas*. *Kāpālikas* and *Pāsupatas* resided and were fed in Siva temples and this led to the establishment of *mathas* in later Pallava times (viz. the Saiva *matha* of Tirumerrali in Kanci) and in early Cola times (viz. the Kalamukha *matha* at Kodumbalur).

The royal patronage of their own temples by the Pallavas was limited in scope. Even the records of the Cola period show few instances of endowments by kings for this royal Pallava institution. It is only in the Vijayanagara grant[22] that we see again a royal order making endowments in land and cash for this temple.

LOCAL PATRONAGE

The patronage by villagers and individuals from areas around the temple comes mainly in the post-Pallava and early-Cola period. We do not get any record inscribed on the walls of the temple, of the Pallava period, which speaks of individual patronage to the temple. Probably this procedure became current only from early Cola times, when we see endowments by private individuals recorded on the walls of the royal temple. The patronage by the *sabhās* of the surrounding villages and by private individuals has been described in detail in the section on cash transactions to the temple. By the early Cola period, it is clear that the Kailasanatha Temple ceased to enjoy its privileged position as a royal temple, and was sustained primarily through the involvement of the local people, i.e. it became a locality temple.

This temple, too, played the traditional role of bringing the various sections of society into closer interaction, though in a limited way. The *manrāḍis* or shepherds were tied to the temple in a service relationship. The local chieftains, like Candraparakrama-vīra, acted as patrons of the temple. The *Brāhmanas* and various groups were closely associated with the temple's functioning. However, its purview was limited in scope as compared to the grandiose designs of the middle Colas.

CONCLUSIONS

Without doubt, it was the Pallavas who initiated the practice of building large-sized temples entirely of stone. What would have prompted Rajasimha to execute such an undertaking? What did the royal temple mean for the Pallavas? Was it an extension of their religious beliefs? Was it an expression of their artistic inclination? Was it a crowning monument to their new concept of kingship or the ritual expression of authority?

THE RELIGIOUS MOTIVE

For the Pallava monarchs, the royal temple was definitely an expression of their religious feelings. It was the Pallavas who were among the first to build temples to their chosen god and name them after themselves. The Kailasanatha temple was originally named the Rajasimhesvara after its builder, Rajasimha. The stamp of the royal patron was forever linked with the name of his god. This practice was introduced in the Tamil country by the Pallavas. The Colas emulated this practice to establish their position as the foremost devotee of their chosen god.

There is no doubt that the Pallavas were influenced by the pervading climate of *bhakti*. Starting with Mahendravarman, who gave up Jainism to embrace Saivism under the influence of Appar the great Saiva saint, and Narasimhavarman or Mamalla, who studded his busy port of Mamallapuram with monolithic temples of immense beauty, the Pallava style of temple-building reached its culmination under Rajasimha. It is believed that the rule of Rajasimha was marked by relative peace; therefore, it was possible for him to devote himself to his great obsession for temple-building. It was under him that the Dravidian style of temple-building reached its maturity. We can state that the Pallavas, and Rajasimha in particular, were the pioneers of a new architectural form. The Pallavas became ardent patrons of temples in a period of intense temple-centred *bhakti* activity, which eulogised kings devoted to either Siva or Visnu and sang the praises of various temples, which became places of pilgrimage. They built temples as a manifestation of their devotion to their chosen god. Therefore, the religious motive in their temple-building activities cannot be overruled. They built temples according to *āgamic* prescriptions with gods facing their prescribed directions. They arranged the temple rituals in accordance with the *āgamas*. Thus, the Pallavas considered themselves a part of the *bhakti* movement in their chosen capacity as temple-builders.

The range of endowments to the temple is not mentioned in the inscs.; neither are details given about the administration of these grants nor the management of the temple. However, from the inscriptional information belonging to a later date, it would appear that the land grants to the temple were not very substantial. The revenue from the grants would have been sufficient in maintaining the temple and its *parivāra*, as well as for conducting the rituals and festivals which were instituted. In other words, they were enough to sustain the temple as a royal religious institution. The interaction with the neighbouring society, if any, was confined to relations with *manradis* and other groups who were involved in a service relationship with the temple. The range of its economic activities and interaction with different sections of society was limited in scope and nature.

It would therefore appear that for the Pallava monarch, the Rajasimhesvara was a royal temple, built with the prime motive of erecting a magnificent monument enconsing the manifestation of the royal ego in the form of the principal deity in the sanctum—the Somaskanda. Siva, Uma and the baby Skanda were said to represent the Pallava monarch, his queen and the prince. The Somaskanda was the deity in all the Pallava royal temples—including the ones in Mamallapuram. This, at a time when the worship of Siva in the form of the *linga* was popular and prevalent all over the Tamil country, indicates an attempt at introducing a new royal cult in the form of Somaskanda. However, this cult did not achieve popular sanction, and the

Somaskanda group of deities was relegated to sub-shrines in later temples and the *linga* was universally accepted as the *mūla-bhēra* in all Siva temples. Even in the Pallava temples, large monolithic *lingas* were installed at a later date, pushing the Somaskanda to the background.

The failure of the Pallavas to establish and popularise their royal cult was avoided by the Middle Cola kings. They did not seek to introduce a new cult in their temples, but adopted and patronised the popular *linga* cult. The *linga* had universal sanction as the aniconic form of Siva. The subtle manner in which the Cola monarchs, after Rajaraja, succeeded in equating the *linga* with the royal ego, is a measure of their shrewd political acumen in transforming a religious symbol to political advantage. (The Colas and the cult of the *linga* will be discussed in the section on Saivism, Ch. II.)

PATRONS OF ART

The Pallavas were great lovers and patrons of art. Among the many titles adopted by Rajasimha was *Atyanta kāma*, a man of limitless desires, which indicates his varied interests. One of his predecessors called himself the *caityakāri* (creator of temples). Sculptural themes found free expression in the cave-temples and bas-reliefs of Mamallapuram. Experimentation in architectural forms was going through an exciting phase. The use of a new medium—stone—for temple-building was proudly proclaimed by Mahendravarman and his successors. Structural temples built entirely of stone, embellished with lion pillars and sculptures came up in place of modest, little shrines made of perishable material. Walls painted with skill surrounded the temples. New iconographical themes were sculpted in the niches of the temples. In short, it was a period of intense artistic achievement in temple-building, sculpture, painting, etc. Rajasimha built the Rajasimhesvara as the pinnacle of his temple-building activities. Thus, for Rajasimha, this temple was an expression of his artistic temperament wherein he gave free play to his imagination by creating and executing a new style in temple-building, embellished with beautiful sculptures and artistic inscs. in the *grantha* script.

PALLAVA CONCEPT OF KINGSHIP

An interesting discussion on the royal temple as a ritual expression of authority is provided by Nicholas Dirks.[23] In his paper, Dirks has traced the role played by the Pallavas as the crucial dynasty in Tamil history which brought about a qualitative change in the concept of kingship. This, in his opinion,

1. Kailasanatha Temple—Kancipuram, Vimana. Courtesy: State Dept. of Archaeology, Tamil Nadu.

2. Tribhuvanam—Kampaharesvara Temple, Vimana. Courtesy: State Dept. of Archaeology, Tamil Nadu.

3. Tiruvarur—Tyagaraja Temple, Gopura. Courtesy: State Dept. of Archaeology, Tamil Nadu.

4. Rajaraja Tiruvasal—Gopura (Brihadisvara Temple).
Courtesy: Gerard Foekema, Amsterdam.

5. Tanjavur—Lower part of Vimana, Brihadisvara Temple (Rajarajesvaram). Courtesy: Gerard Foekema, Amsterdam.

6. Tanjavur—Vimana, Brihadisvara Temple (Rajarajesvaram).
Courtesy: Gerard Foekema, Amsterdam.

created new political alliances with intermediary chiefs. The Pallava king, through his acts of *dāna* in granting *brahmadēyas* to Brahmanas and through his temple-building activities, proclaimed himself the foremost granter of gifts. This, in turn, enhanced his importance and the sanctity of his family.

In the early stages it was only the king and his immediate royal retinue who could make endowments. Gradually, in the period under discussion, we find at first royal and military officers with the title of *ajñapati* or executor of grants. More importantly, a new category appeared, that of the *vijñapati* or petitioner of grants. The *vijñapati*, usually an important local chieftain or headman, petitioned the king for the right to give the grant himself. The *vijñapati* was also eulogised in the very same manner as the king and represented "an order of magnitude previously embodied only in the king and his family. The expression of the political system was such that the king was now able to establish relations with individuals who either did not exist before, or who had previously been either rivals or allies....It was in this capacty that the ritual of the royal *dāna* proclaimed the basis of sovereignty and established authoritative relations with loyal subordinates."

The occasion for the gift was marked by grants (mostly on copper-plates) which were used to proclaim the divine genealogies of the Pallavas, which, in turn, became the base of sovereignty for the Pallava family. It is probably for these very reasons that the Pallavas viewed the temples differently from the Colas. It is also probably the reason why they inscribed their *biruḍas* and exploits on the walls of their temples, and left out mundane information like administrative details. It was a period of the consolidation of the concept of divine kingship, a precursor to the concept of the *dēvrāja.*

The Rajasimhesvara was thus an exclusive royal monument built to glorify the king and his family and their royal cult of Somaskanda. It was in all respects a royal temple built as an expression of the king's monarchical aspirations and exclusiveness. It was a monument truly reflecting the religious sentiments expressed by the contemporary *bhakti* saints. By shrewdly naming the temple after him, and by inscribing his titles, Rajasimha sought to project himself as a true devotee dedicating all his desires and aspirations to Him. We see this temple as a forerunner of the Great Temple of Rajaraja, but the latter expanded its potentialities far beyond its religious dimensions and converted the royal temple into an institution of royal power.

REFERENCES

1. SII, I, 86.
2. SII, I, 24-30.
3. SII, II, pt. IV, Addenda, Kuram Grant.
4. C. Minakshi, Pallava Administration, Ch. X.
5. SII, II, 84.
6. SII, I, 86.
7. SII, II, 78.
8. Ibid, 86.
9. SII, I, 149
10. Ibid, 86.
11. Ibid, 84.
12. Ibid, 85.
13. Ibid, Nos. 146-48.
14. Ibid, 82, 83.
15. SII, XII, 69.
16. C. Minakshi, op. cit., Ch. XII.
17. SII, I, pt. IV.
18. Ibid, 86.
19. C. Minakshi, op. cit., Ch. XII.
20. SII, I, 88.
21. Muktesvara Temple, op. cit.
22. SII, I, 86.
23. Nicholas B. Dirks, "Political Authority and Structural Change in Early South Indian History".

Chapter II

THE RAJARAJESVARAM THE ROYAL TEMPLE OF RAJARAJA

INTRODUCTION

With the accession of Rajaraja I, Cola history enters a century of grandeur and glory. Inheriting a relatively small kingdom, ravaged by the Rastrakuta invasion, Rajaraja had, by the end of his reign, expanded the frontiers of his kingdom and laid the foundations of a well-knit empire. Not only was he a great conqueror, but his singular achievement lay in creating an administrative machinery which brought vast territories together. In this, he was ably assisted by a loyal army. In almost every field of statecraft, the stamp of Rajaraja's genius and grandiose vision is evident—be it in his military exploits which extended the empire across the seas to Sri Lanka in the South and to the Telugu and Kannada countries in the North; be it in the size and complex organisation of his administration; be it in his patronage to Saivism and to Tamil literature; be it in art and architecture, etc. In everything, we see "at work powerful forces newly liberated by the progressive imperialism of the time".[1] Much has been written about his nobility when he made way for his uncle to ascend the Cola throne instead of staking his own claim to it; and about his obedience and devotion to his grand-aunt, Sembiyam Madevi. It is said that under her advice and influence he undertook to build a great temple to Siva in his capital city of Tanjavur.

By far, his greatest achievement which immortalised him for all time to come was his monumental temple to Siva, which he named the Rajarajesvaram after himself. Built to sanctify his capital city of Tanjavur, the Rajarajesvaram (known in present times as the Brihadisvara or just as the Big

Temple) in size and reach was the most magnificent edifice of its time. Compared to it, the other temples were like little village churches before a cathedral. The eleventh century was the grandest period of temple-building activity in India. It was this century which witnessed the construction of the Khandariya Mahadeva and other temples at Khajuraho; the Lingaraja Temple at Bhuvanesvar and the Osian Temples of Rajasthan. None of these great temples could however measure up to the grandeur of the Rajarajesvaram, which has been called 'Devalaya Chakravarti of Indian Temples' by S.R. Balasubramaniam.[2]

The Rajarajesvaram was built entirely during the lifetime of Rajaraja himself. Started in the year 1003 A.D., Rajaraja consecrated the temple with a copper-pot (*kalaśa*), meant to serve as the finial at the top of the *vimāna*, in the 25th year of his reign (1009-10 A.D.). In his 29th year, he engraved on the temple walls the elaborate administrative and financial procedures of the temple. Built entirely of stone, quarried and brought from a considerable distance, the Great Temple is a fitting tribute to the Dravidian *sthapati's* skill. It was the richest temple of its time. The king and his royal entourage lavished their wealth on it. The quantum of gold gifted to the temple amounted to over 41,500 *kaḻañjus*; 50,650 *kaḻañjus* of silver; and jewels valued at 10,200 *kāśus* were also gifted. The revenue from land grants yielded an annual income of more than 145,889 *kalams* of paddy, and cash income amounted to 1,308 *kāśus*. Almost 800 persons were in the employ of the temple as full-time functionaries. They were given attractive perquisites in the form of land grants, houses and cash.

The temple complex covers an overall area of 240.79m East to West and 121.92m North to South. Surrounded by a vast courtyard (*tiruch-chuṟṟu-māligai*) there are two walls—the outer wall being a defensive one with bastions. It was called the Krishnan Raman *tiruch-chuṟṟu-māligai*, after his commander-in-chief, who got it built. This is the first instance of defence works in any South Indian temple. The sanctum is built on a basement measuring 5m in height. Over this base rises the towering structure of the *srivimana* of thirteen storeys (*talas*). The *srivimana* is topped by a single block of granite of 7.77m sq.

Rajaraja built the temple complex complete with additional shrines for Candesvara and Nandi-mandapa, eight shrines for the *dikpālas*, shrine for the royal preceptor, Karur Devar and the two walls surrounded by a moat. The shrines for Amman, Ganesa and Subrahmanya were later additions. The simple, unitary and yet majestic plan of the complex speaks volumes of the aesthetic taste of its creator, Rajaraja and the religious cults which he renewed and incorporated in the complex.

It was not just a masterpiece of South Indian temple architecture, but the manner in which arrangements were made for managing the affairs of the temple and for recording on its walls all the information regarding its administration and grants, is eloquent testimony of his meticulous attention to details. The temple, in every respect, became a model for the future. The Great Temple was the jewel that adorned the capital city of the greatest monarch of Southern India. The range of its contacts was much wider than that of an average temple; but almost every temple, however small in size and restricted in influence, was a miniature of the Great Temple and had its counterpart of every feature of the larger institution.

In the following sections, the various facets of this temple are discussed in detail. From this study we can have an appreciation of the vision of Rajaraja in creating this unique royal institution. We see the manner in which he used this temple as an important arm of the royal government to exercise royal authority over the entire empire. It was truly a novel concept to use a religious institution like the Brahmanical Temple to help consolidate Cola hegemony over vast conquered territories.

SECTION I

ADMINISTRATIVE SET-UP OF THE ROYAL TEMPLE

The Rajarajesvaram of Tanjavur provides us with one of the most detailed lists of temple authorities/functionaries. The manner in which the arrangements for its administration were made, and the minute details that were attended to, bespeak of the efficient and tight administrative machinery of the Colas under Rajaraja and his son, Rajendra. It is possible that the administration of this temple was initially based on the existing administrative set-up of smaller shrines in the Cola region. However, the administration of this temple was more elaborate and completely under the control of the royal government. In order to maintain such a large establishment, extensive endowments in land and cash were made. The king set apart lands in several villages throughout his dominions, including Sri Lanka, to yield an annual income of more than 145,889 *kalams* of paddy and cash income of more than 1,308 *kāśus.* Therefore, it was seen that the revenue and other dues of the temple from these far-off places were efficiently collected. The temple had a staff of almost 800 persons. Revenue administration and personnel management were the important functions of the royal temple.

Bhakti temples were administered and managed for the most part by trustees from among the people. They were, thus, usually independent of royal interference. On the other hand, the Big Temple was totally a creation of the religious fervour and power of the king. It was created by a monarch to enhance his glory and was managed by him and his royal officials who utilised the vast resources from their various conquests to make it the richest shrine of its time. "The systematic way in which the various endowments to the temple were made and the principles laid down for their proper administration bespeak a genius for organisation which could not have been quite a characteristic feature of kings in general at the time."[3]

Studies on temple administration have usually divided the role of the functionaries under three heads: secular, spiritual/religious and quasi-religious. This classification is more from the point of convenience, as very often there is overlapping of duties between secular and religious administration. Despite the fact that the administrative model of most temples followed on established lines, still the varieties of duties performed by each functionary in different temples is baffling to say the least. In the earlier period, when most temples were administered by *sabhās* and their committees, the ambiguity in functions was not so pronounced. Whereas in the period of the Tanjavur temple, the temple administration had broken free of local assembly control and was more or less autonomous. Despite this, it is to be noted that no two temples followed a uniform pattern of administration. In some temples the spiritual heads undertook the trusteeship of the endowments;[4] in others it was the *dēvakanmis*—the executive officers of the temple—who were the recipients of gifts made to the temples.[5] In the Vaidyanathasvami Temple at Tirumalavadi, the *śrikāryam* is said to be an officer who was virtually a priest in the temple in charge of worship.[6] Whereas in the Tanjavur temple, the *śrikāryam* officer is the secular manager who does not appear to interfere in spiritual matters.

Thus when we analyse the administrative pattern of the Tanjavur temple, we have to treat it as an individual case. Perhaps Rajaraja tried to improve upon or rectify the shortcomings in the administration in other temples. Even so, we must bear in mind the priorities and compulsions of administering a large, royal temple would have been different. The influences on the king from spiritual preceptors and *rājagurus* were considerable for him to give enough importance to these dignitaries in the affairs of the royal temple. The *rājaguru* on the other hand would not have had such an important and influential role in other temples. Their influence was duplicated in most temples by the *maṭhādipatis* (heads of *maṭhas*), who were gradually gaining control over temples replacing the *sabhās* in their management.

In the Tanjavur temple, according to B. Venkatraman,[7] three names are important:

(a) Adityan Suryan, alias Tennavan *muvendavelan*, who was the headman of Poygai Nāḍu. He was the *śrikāryam* officer of the temple during Rajaraja's as well as Rajendra's time. We do not hear of any other *śrikāryam* officer after him.

(b) Karūr-Dēvar was the spiritual preceptor of Rajaraja I. It is said that on his advice, Rajaraja agreed to build a great temple to Siva. He was a *Siva yōgin* and thus revered as a holy person. He is said to have helped in fixing the *linga* in the *āvuḍaiyār* at the time of consecrating the Great Temple. Among the murals on the inner walls of the temple is a portrait, said to be of the king with his preceptor, Karūr Dēvar. He has sung the praises of Lord Brihadisvara (Rajarajesvara) in his poetical composition, Tiruviśaippa. His *samādhi* is in the outer courtyard of the temple.

(c) The heads of the Golaki *maṭha* were the chief priests of the temple. Guru Īśāna Śiva Pandita was the chief priest during Rajaraja's time. He and his successors were the chief priests of the temple and were in charge of the *āgamic* conduct of worship as well as of the endowments of the temple.

Following on traditional lines, this study also divides the administration into secular, religious and quasi-religious. But this, as already stated, is more for the sake of convenience. For it will be seen that certain functionaries performed both religious and secular functions. Therefore, it will be wrong to think that we can study the role of functionaries by dividing them into watertight compartments.

SECULAR ADMINISTRATION

In the case of the royal temple of Rajarajesvaram, the royal officers and the other officials in charge of the secular administration of the temple were all government appointees.

Tānattārs: This was the traditional name for the trustees of a temple. Though the Big Temple was under royal control, the daily affairs of the temple would have to be managed by a group of trustees. It is not stated explicitly as to who were the members who constituted this executive body of trustees. In all likelihood, the trustees would be the manager, the chief priest, the executive officers and the accountants. A reference to the *tānattārs* is found in a later record of Tribhuvana Cakravartin Konerimaikondan[8] who built the shrine of Brihannayaki in this temple; and in his second year presented the shrine with eleven *vēli* of land in a village. This order belongs to the late 13th c., and was addressed to the authorities (*tānattārs*) of the temple, and was signed by the headman (*uḍaiyār*) of Kodumbalur and Kayalur. This seems to be the only known record mentioning the *tānattār*. A previous record refers to a royal order being addressed to the manager, the chief priest and the executive officers of the temple. However, they are not referred to as the *tānattārs*. It is likely that the inscriptional reference to *tānattār* was not made during Rajaraja's time. It is likely that after Rajaraja's period when royal patronage and personnel were withdrawn, the administration was entrusted to a body of independent trustees (*tānattārs*). During the rule of Rajaraja and that of his son, Rajendra, decisions regarding the royal temple would have been taken directly by the royal government.

Śrikāryam: This term is very often used to denote the officer *Śrikāryam Śeyvār.*[9] The word means one who was the executive officer of the temple and who executed the decisions of the *tānattārs.* The *śrikāryam* was in charge of the day-to-day management of the temple.

Many records tell us that the *śrikāryam* was authorised to supervise the proper conduct of worship and related matters. In some temples, the *śrikāryam* officers seemed to be subordinate to the other officers. They undertook to look after temple properties like land, and pay the requisite taxes to the state.[10] They recorded the grants[11] and looked after temple personnel.[12] They seem to have been paid by way of land or grain.[13] Thus, in most temples, they were paid officers under the control of the *tānattārs.*

However in the Tanjavur temple, the *śrikāryam* was the most important administrative officer. Only important officials and high dignitaries were appointed as the *śrikāryam* in Cola times. The *śrikāryam* was generally responsible for the implementation of endowments. Royal orders for remunerating temple officials were addressed to the temple manager and the accountants.

In the Rajarajesvaram, the *śrikāryam* officer seems to have been only in charge of secular duties. As already stated, the *śrikāryam* in some temples were the chief priests. Perhaps Rajaraja realized the importance of appointing an administrative head, independent of spiritual duties. In such a large temple as the Rajarajesvaram with a staff of 800, it must have been a very important and coveted post. The appointment of temple personnel, their remuneration, the receipt and execution of endowments were under the *śrikāryam* officer. As a royal officer who was the administrative head of the most important royal temple in the Cola country, he would have helped the government in fixing the salaries and perquisites of various temple staff. Even in later times, royal orders for remunerating temple officials were addressed to the temple manager and the accountants.

In the Rajarajesvaram, the *śrikāryam* was Adityan Suryan. The title mūvendavelan suggests that he was a high official of considerable means. He has made several endowments in cash and kind to the temple. One inscription[14] says that Adityan Suryan made 2 deposits of money, which were lent out to the inhabitants of a certain village. The interest on the deposit was used for procuring articles of consumption on 13 yearly procession days. He set up 7 images before the 29th year of Rajaraja and presented them with a number of ornaments.[15] Inscs. Nos. 40, 41, 60 of SII, II, mention various gifts to the temple by the same manager. Among the solid images set up by him were those of the Saiva saints, as well as those of Periya Perumal (Rajaraja I) and his consort Ulōgamadeviyar (Lōka Mahadevi). He also set up images of different aspects of Siva as Bhairava, Chandrasekhara etc. This same manager is mentioned in several inscriptions even of the time of Rajendra I. No other *śrikāryam* of this temple is mentioned. Therefore, it is likely that Adityan Suryan continued to be the *śrikāryam* during the entire short period of this temple's glory. There is no mention anywhere about his salary or any *kāṇi* grant made to him. As already stated, Adityan Suryan was the headman of a village and as such an important landholder. The appointment to the *śrikāryam* of the Rajarajesvaram was a prestigious post with considerable power and influence.

Head Overseer (*Kaṇkāṇi-nāyagam*): A record[16] describes the gift of a brass spittoon to an image of Pillaiyar Ganapati by the chief manager of the Rajarajesvaram Temple. It says, "Aravanai, alias (Ma)1-Ari-kesavan, the headman of Palur in Pandi-nāḍu, who held the office of head-overseer (*kaṇkāṇi-nāyagam*) of the management of the temple (*śrikāryam*) of the Lord Sri-Rajarajesvara...." That this manager belonged to a village in Pandi nāḍu would mean that, being an efficient administrator, he was transferred to the capital city. Having conquered vast areas, the Cola kings could draw upon the best talents in the empire. The word *'kankani'* means a supervisor who carries out the orders or supervises the execution of works on behalf of the temple manager. He was probably subordinate to the *śrikāryam* and acted as a link between the service-holders or workers and the management.

Accountants (*Karanattār*): Candesvara was the saint in whose name the monetary affairs of the temple were transacted. He was the housekeeper or 'Major Domo' of the temple, the Adi-Dasa, or original servant of Siva.[17] It was in his name that money was received or given out. The accountants or *karanattār* were very important officers of the administration. They maintained the temple accounts (*kaṇakkeḻuda*). The money donated by the king, his queens, his sister and his officers were lent out to villages at an annual interest of 12%.

A record of Rajaraja[18] speaks of a royal order to the inhabitants of the *brahmadēyas* in Colamandalam, Pandimandalam and Tondaimandalam to supply permanently to the Tanjavur temple many important officials. The order states that these *brahmadēyas* should supply to the temple.

(a) as temple treasurers, *Brāhmanas* in those *brahmadēyas*, who are rich in land, connections or capital;

(b) *Brahmacārins* (*maṇi*) as temple servants;

(c) Accountants for writing accounts (of the temple).

In all were listed 14 accountants and 8 junior accountants. Each accountant along with his assistants could have been in charge of one aspect of the financial transactions of the temple. All royal orders were conveyed to them. Each accountant was paid 200 *kalams* of paddy a year by the temple measure, Ādavallan. The junior accountant received 75 *kalams* a year. This order also states that the treasurers and the accountants should receive their allowances at the up-country treasury of the temple (*nāṭṭu-bhandāram*). The record states specifically that these posts could be filled only by Brahmanas of some financial standing, and not by a person who would have to depend solely on his earnings from the temple. This might be to eliminate petty corruption in a temple of such vast resources and wealth. Generally, the temple accountants were in charge of the income and expenditure of the temples. In a temple like the Rajarajesvaram, the accountants were in charge of income to the tune of 60,000 *kāśus* a year.

Treasurers (*Bhandārattār*): In all, four treasurers were listed in the Tanjavur temple. They were appointed in the same way as the accountants and were probably paid the same salary too.

The grants and gifts were entered in the treasury register (*bhandāra-pottakam*) by the treasurers.[19] Thereafter, they were deposited in the safe vaults of the temple. Initially, the nature of their functions appeared to make them a receiving and distributing body.[20] Later, with the increase in the wealth of temples, the treasurers became members of the administrative body of temples. There are inscriptional references to '*poṇbandāram*'[21] for gold deposits and jewellery. The *Bhandārattār* protected the temple charities and the maintenance of its services. The treasurers measured out the required quantity of rice and other items for the conduct of *pūjās* and festivals. Land grants were also entrusted to them. Important documents were kept in the temple treasury; and the *bhandāram* acted as a bank in times of need. The staff of the

Big Temple were instructed to draw their respective salaries in the form of paddy or cash from two treasuries, the *nāṭṭu-bhandāram* and the *uḷḷūr-bhandāram*. This way Rajaraja ensured that the pressure of work was equally distributed.

Officer in charge of Paddy Supply: An insc.[22] of 1116 A.D. of Vikrama Choladeva states that the king assigned an allowance to a person who measured paddy in the Tanjavur temple and the villages belonging to it. This man was evidently a controlling officer who had to check supplies of paddy which had to be delivered into the temple stores. It goes on to state that the king ordered an allowance "which was permanently enjoyed by his grandfather, as an allowance for measuring paddy (*kar*) to Rajaraja-Pallavarayan, who measures paddy in the temple of Lord Rajarajesvaram". He was given one share or paddy equal to one *vēli* of land, i.e. 100 *kalams* a year. That the grandfather of this officer was on the staff of the Big Temple, means that even in Rajaraja's time such an appointment was made.

Master of Rent Roll: A record[23] speaks of a gift to the shrine of Ganapatiyar by a servant of Rajaraja. This donor was apparently employed in the department which regulated the levying of taxes from endowments—a master of rent roll in the department (*tiṅaikkalam*) of taxes levied from endowments.

Dēvakanmis: S.R. Balasubramanian thinks that they were priests;[24] but most scholars are of the opinion that the *dēvakanmis* were executive officers of the temple. K.V. Subramaniya Aiyer[25] and others have classified them as superintendents or managers of temples. K.V. Soundararajan[26] thinks that they were trustees of temples. The reason for this ambiguity in classifying them may be due to the variegated roles that they played in different temples. In most temples, though, they were the executive officers,[27] receiving gifts; accepting gold coins for expenditure; distributing livestock and collecting the requisite quantity of ghee, milk, etc.; paying taxes for the lands donated to the temple; taking charge of lands in order to offer holy feeding on the king's natal star; feeding *śivayōgins* and *māhēśvaras* on festival days, etc. All these duties were discharged by the *dēvakanmis* as mentioned in the records of the Tirumalvadi Temple.

Although it is not explicitly stated in the records of the Tanjavur Temple, it is likely that the *dēvakanmis* performed similar duties in the royal temple, too. The record of 1116 A.D.[28] speaks of the royal order being addressed to the manager, the *pañcācāryas* and the *dēvakanmis* of the temple.

They were a party to most of the important transactions of the temple. From this it is obvious that they combined in themselves the various duties mentioned above. Their independence in decision-making was restricted, as they usually functioned with the other officials. Their number is not specified in any record nor is the manner of their appointment mentioned.

The order of Vikrama Cola has been translated into English by Hultzsch as being addressed to the manager, the *pañcācāryas* and the *dēvakanmis* of the temple. He has interpreted *dēvakanmis* as *pūjāris*. Thus, three persons/groups have been listed by him. However, the insc. in Tamil lists only two, viz. *'śrikārya seyyavanukkum, pariyāramuḷ paṭṭuḍai-pañcācārya-dēvakanigaḷukkum'*. The *pañcācāryas* and the *dēvakanmis* have been grouped as one body. This is significant, as *dēvakanmis* are a recognised group of executive officers in most temples. They are rarely known to be associated with the spiritual side of temples. However, priests like the Pancacaryas were associated not only with religious matters, but also with grants/endowments. That these two well-defined groups have been addressed as one is interesting, as it could be interpreted both ways, i.e. the *pañcācāryas* were also executive officers or that the executive officers (*dēvakanmis*) also officiated as priests.

Engraver of inscriptions (*Mēykritis*): The 'Imperial' Colas gave considerable importance to engraving *mēykritis*, in order to establish and proclaim their suzerainty over other areas. In a new insc.[29] discovered in the northern enclosure wall behind the Amman shrine in the Rajarajesvaram, mention is made of the officer entrusted with the responsibility of getting the inscs. engraved in the Big Temple at Tanjavur. It says: *"uḍaiyar-kōyilil eḻuttu veṭṭurikkinra-Arumoḻidēvavalanāṭṭu vandaraivēlūrk-kuṟṟattu śāttankuḍi vēḷḷālan Iṛavipalūr-uḍaiyār"*.

Superintendent of Temple Women: Mention is made of two officials to supervise the work of the temple women and the female musicians (*Gāndharvi*).[30] The insc. states: *Tali chchērippenḍugaḷukkum-Gāndharvigaḷukkum-Nāyakkaṅ Seyya.* They received two shares each. Each share (*pangu*) was the produce of one *vēli* of land, calculated at 100 *kalams* of paddy. One of them was called Savur Paranjodi after a Saiva devotee who was a contemporary of Tirunanasambandar and Narasimha Pallava I.

Watchmen (*Tirumēykkāpu*): A royal order of the 29th year of Rajaraja[31] says that the *brahmadēyas* in Colamandalam should supply the Tanjavur temple with watchmen; and that they should pay them annually 100 *kalams* each out of the tax dues of the village. Apart from this, daily allowances (*paḍi*) had to be paid by the respective villages out of their tax dues. This is an example of an indirect remission of taxes by the government in favour of the royal temple. Two inscs. give the names of villages which had to supply watchmen to the temple. There were 143 watchmen in all. Most villages had to supply only one watchman; in some rare cases two or more watchmen were supplied by a single village. These were usually *taniyūrs*, considered to be larger economic units than average villages. For example, "members of the assembly of Rajasraya CVM in Uraiyur Kurram (a sub-division of Keralantaka Valanāḍu) have to supply 2 temple watchmen". Another *taniyūr*, Sri Viranarayana CVM, in Nallarrur nāḍu supplied as many as 6 watchmen. The income of this *taniyūr* might have been six times that of an average *brahmadēya* village.

The 143 watchmen enumerated would have been, no doubt, assigned to different parts of the temple and it is possible that they were organised into various units. Thus, it is likely that these watchmen would have constituted the various watchmen units mentioned in Rajendra I's insc.[32] They were called *Keralāntaka-Vāsal-tiru-mēykappār; Keralāntaka-terinda-parivārattar; Singaḷāntaka-terinda-parivārattar; Jananātha-terinda-parivārattar; Anukka-vāsal-tirumēykāppār* and *Parivāra-mēykāppārgaḷ of Teṇkaraināḍu*. These groups were made responsible for the services to some of the images set up in the temple.

Tiruvāykēḷvi: This literally means one who proclaims the sacred commands of the God. This person deposited 40 *kāśus* which were lent out on interest to the village of Sri Viranarayana CVM.

SPIRITUAL FUNCTIONARIES

Śaivācārya: The *śaivācāryas* of the Golaki *maṭha* were the *rāja-gurus* of the 'Imperial' Colas. They were also the *dīkśa gurus* of the Kalachuris, Kakatiyas, the Malvas and the Telugu Colas. Guru Īśāna-Śiva Pandita was the *rāja-guru* of Rajaraja. He was one of the most important functionaries of the Rajarajesvaram. He was succeeded by Śaivācārya Pavana Pidaran and by Śaivācārya Sarva Siva Pandita during the reign of Rajendra I. Svāmidēva Śri Kaṇṭha-Śiva was the *guru* of Vikrama Cola; Sōmēśvara of Kulottunga III, etc. Rajendra I is credited with an endowment[33] of an *ācāryabhōga* for Śaivācārya Sarva Siva Pandita and his deserving pupils (*śisyas*) and their pupils (*praśisyas*) who were natives of Aryadesa, Madhyadesa and Gaudadesa. According to this grant, 2000 *kalams* of paddy a year, measured by the *marakkaḷ* in the temple, should be supplied to the treasury of the city for the purpose. Sastri states[34] that the entire charity of the temple was under the Saivacaryas of the family of Sarva-Siva.

It was under the influence and guidance of these *gurus* that the Cola kings built great temples dedicated to Siva, strictly following Saiva *āgamas*. The *śaivācāryas* ensured that worship (*pūjā*) was conducted according to *āgamic* rules. The *śaivācāryas*, therefore, supervised the conduct of spiritual matters in the temples.

However, the *śaivācārya* of the Big Temple was not just a spiritual head. Considerable endowments of the temple were under the control of the *śaivācārya*. All royal orders were addressed to the manager, the *śaivācārya* and the executive officers. Thus, the *śaivācārya* had administrative duties for safeguarding certain categories of endowments of the temple.

The esteem in which the *śaivācāryas* were held is evident by the small sculptures of the images of 108 *śaivācāryas* found carved in a row in the Rajarajesvaram at Darasuram. Guru Isana Siva commanded power and wealth as the Chief Priest of Rajaraja. He donated 8 gilt copper pots and made several cash deposits in the temple. He set up an image (*pratima*) of himself in the temple and donated money for a lamp to his image: "To the shepherd...were assigned 32 *kāśus* out of the money deposited by the priest (*gurukkal*) Īśāna Śiva Pandita for a lamp to the image of the *gurukkal* set up in the temple."[35]

Māhēśvaras: They were Saiva devotees, who took active interest in the administration of Siva temples (like the *Srivaiśnava* in the case of Visnu temples). S.R. Balasubramaniam says they were temple trustees,[36] with similar responsibility as the *dēvakanmis*. The *paṇ-māhēśvaras'* protection is invoked at the end of inscs. Many of the powers and responsibilities of the *māhēśvaras* are not mentioned in the records of the Rajarajesvaram. The role of the *māhēśvaras* (as also that of other functionaries) must have been well-understood by all to necessitate putting them down on record. There were several *māhēśvaras* and they were under a head, known as *māhēśvara-kankāṇi*.

Pañcācāryas: The priests attached to temples organised themselves into groups with many picturesque names. The generic name for these priestly groups of Saivas was *śivabrāhmanas*. The *pañcācāryas* were *ādi-śivas*, who performed the actual *pūjā*. Their first emanation was from Agastya, Kasyapa, Gautama, Bharadvaja and Kausika. In due course, *pañcācāryas* had different names which were based on their *dīkśa*. These five names were Īśāna, Tatpuruśa, Aghōra, Vāmadeva and Sadyōjāta.

The Tanjavur insc. of 1116 A.D.[37] refers to them as '*pariyāramūla paṭṭuḍai pañcācārya-dēvarkanmigaḷukkum*'. As stated earlier it refers to the *pañcācāryas* and the *dēvakanmis* as a common body. Thus, the *pañcācāryas* were groups who were entrusted with managing endowments. No mention is made of the payment to these groups of priests. The temple priest had also several perquisites over and above his salary. A part of their money was received from Candesvara and a part from the *sirudanattu paṇimakkaḷ* (servants of the minor treasure).

Brahmacārins: They were bachelor temple servants. They wore a single garment, sported a small tuft of hair, smeared their bodies with sacred ash, had deerskin tied to their sacred thread and wore rings of green, coarse grass.[38] The royal order[39] belonging to the 29th year of Rajaraja to the inhabitants of Colamandalam, Pandimandalam and Tondaimandalam, that they had to supply permanently to the Tanjavur temple, among others, Brahmacarins, who were temple servants, lists 178 Brahmacarins (*mani*) in all. Each Brahmacarin temple servant was to get 1 *padakku* paddy daily plus 4 *kāśus* yearly. They were to receive their allowance of paddy and *kāśu* at the city treasury of the temple. Some villages had to send only one temple servant; others more. Among these, to each of ten who had taken permanent vows (*ēkāṅgis*)—3 *kuruṇi* paddy per day plus 4 *kāśus* yearly. To another set of 20 Brahmacarins (the qualifications are obliterated), one *padakku* paddy per day plus 5 *kāśus* per year.

Brahmacarins had the job of reciting *Vēdic* mantras for different functions and helping in the preparation of the *pūjās* etc. They could never perform the actual *pūjā* though. They performed duties like carrying holy water for bathing the deity, lighting the lamps, preparing the *pūjā* items and other such jobs. In such a large temple as the Rajarajesvaram, with several *pūjās* performed daily and several festivals annually, a large contingent of temple servants was required.

Śiva Yōgins: They were holy men who were adept at yoga processes according to *āgamic* principles. Karūr Dēvar was a Śiva Yōgin, and a person of considerable influence in the royal temple of Rajarajesvaram. There were 240 Śiva Yōgins in the temple who had to be fed on 24 festival days, in the hall (*sālai*) of the temple. For this purpose 25 *kalam* paddy per year was set aside for one meal for each of the Śiva Yōgins.

Tirupadiyam Vinnappam Seyvar:[40] There were 48 persons to recite and sing the *Tēvaram* in the temple, and 2 persons who accompanied them on the drums. These 48 chorists (*Pidarar*) and 2 drummers received from the city treasury a daily allowance (*nibandha*) of 3 *kuruni* (24 measures) paddy each, measured by the *marakkāl* (*Ādavallan*). All the persons of the choir including the drummers had aliases ending in 'Siva'.

Āriyam Singers:[41] Singers in Sanskrit who received 150 *kalams* of paddy a year each were appointed to the royal temple. Rajaraja encouraged the recitation of Sanskrit verses (probably Vedic slokas).

QUASI-RELIGIOUS FUNCTIONARIES

Devaradiyār (Temple Women): One of the most important inscs. in the Big Temple is a royal order belonging to the 29th year of Rajaraja.[42] It speaks of the appointment of 400 dancing girls to the Tanjavur temple from other temples and religious centres of Colamandalam. As many as 91 temples located in 52 different villages in Colamandalam contributed these temple women, some of them as many as 5 to 8. These temple women were called *devaradiyār* or in some places *taḷip-pendir.* Each person received one share (consisting of the produce of one *vēli* of land, calculated at 100 *kalams* of paddy), plus one house in the two streets newly formed, and called '*Teṛkku*' and '*Vaḍakku' telich-chēri* (the south and north temple streets). It states further that in the event of the death of any one of them, the nearest relation of this person, found suitable, should receive the share and discharge the ordained duty.

The duties of these *taḷip-pendir* are not specified in the records of the Big Temple. Probably they were well-established and too well-known to need mention. Therefore, we have to look elsewhere to know what kind of work was expected from temple women.[43] By and large, they were dancers attached to the deity. They danced before the deities at stipulated times, especially when the deity was taken out on festival days. In course of time, they became courtesans, who became favourites of kings and nobles. Several of them became very wealthy due to their royal or noble connections. Some of them made lavish contributions to temples and built *mandapams* and set up idols (as mentioned in the Ch. on Tiruvarur). Many of them were given temple honours and received respect from society. That most of them were dancers is clear from the appointment of 6 dancing masters (receiving two shares each) to the Tanjavur temple.[44]

The *dēvaradiyār* have been described variously as *dēvadāsis, teḷippendir* or simply as temple women. Among the various duties performed by these women was the duty of husking the paddy.[45] The Rajarajesvaram had a large granary which could stock more than one lakh *kalams* of paddy intended for food offerings and other services. Some women did duty on a hereditary basis. The cleaning and decoration of temple premises and the gathering of flowers as well as making of garlands must also have been among the duties performed by these temple women. However, the most important duty expected of them was as temple dancers and singers.

Nivendakkārar: Those servants who received an allowance (*nibandha*) were called Nivendakkarar. This insc.[46] from the Rajarajesvaram gives the names and details of several temple servants. The details of remuneration of these servants and their number are given systematically in this very long insc.:

1. 6 Nos. dance masters got two shares each. They are called *naṭṭuvancheyya naṭṭuvān*. One of them is called Mummadi Solanrittamārāyan (great king of the dancers of Mummadicola).
2. 4 Nos. drama directors who received 1 share each.
3. 3 Nos. singers of the Vēdas (*Āriyam*), received 2 shares each.
4. 4 singers of the *Tēvaram*, received 1 share each.
5. 3 Nos. pipe players (*vaṅgiyam*), received 1 share each. Some of them were from army regiments like the *nigarili-sōḻa-terinda-udanilar-kudirai chchēvagai* (chosen horsemen of the retinue of Nigarilichola).
6. 4 Nos. musicians called Vādyamārāyan, received 2 shares each.
7. 2 Nos. drummers who beat the small drum (*uśukkai*) received 1 share each.
8. 2 Nos. who played the lute (*vīṇai*). In the event of the death of one of them, his share had to go to his uncle's son who was married to his daughter. They received 3 shares. This is an example of the meticulous detail of administrative arrangements in the temple. It shows that every appointee was hand-picked.
9. 3 Nos. who sang in Sanskrit (*Āriyam*) and received 1 share each.
10. 4 Nos. who sang in Tamil—1 share each.
11. 2 Nos. players of the big drum (*koṭṭimattaḷam*)—1 share each.

12. 2 Nos. conch-blowers (*muttirai-sangu*)—1 share each. One of them was taken from *mummadi-sōḻa-terinda-ānaippāgan* (the elephant riders of Mummadi Sola). This is an example of musicians attached to regiments, who gave service in the royal temple during peace time.
13. 1 No. drummer from Tanjavur—1 share.
14. 5 Nos. *pakkavādyar*—3/4 share each.
15. 3 Nos. musicians (*gāndharvar*)—3/4 share each.
16. 22 drummers from various temples and military troops like the Parantaka Kongaval (the Kongu soliders of Parantaka) etc.
17. 5 Nos. who proclaim the sacred commands of the god (*tiruvāykēlvi*)—1 share each. One of them, i.e. Rajakesari Kodandaraman, alias Jayankonda Sola-Kadigaimarayan, was a donor in insc. No. 25.
18. 66 Nos. drummers who received 1/2 share each.

Apart from these servants, there were sacred parasol-bearers, lamp lighters, sprinklers of water, *cannaliyal* (?), potters, washermen, *kavidi*, barbers, astrologers, tailors, jewel-stitcher, brazier, master carpenter and his assistants, *paṇas*, superintendents of goldsmiths etc. The total number of functionaries numbered more than 800.

Actors: An insc. of Rajendradeva[47] says that a daily allowance of paddy should be paid to a troop of actors who performed a drama called 'Rajarajesvaranataka' in the temple on the occasion of the Vaikāṣi festival. They were to be paid at the rate of 1 *tuni* of paddy per day for the actor (*sānti-kūttan*) and members of his troop (*varga*) equal to 120 *kalams* paddy a year. This order was conveyed to the temple manager and accountants and signed by the royal secretary.

Free-Labour: A record[48] states that a certain Mallappa-Nayakkar ordered the inhabitants of the village of Puliyur to build the *mantapa* which adjoins the Brihannayaki shrine and that he rewarded their services by assigning to them the remnants of the offerings to the goddess. Although Appadorai identifies them as slaves, it is doubtful if we can call them so. In many cases widows and others spent their life in the temple service as an act of piety.

CONDITIONS OF WORK

Many of the *nivēndakkārar* like the dancers and male servants held hereditary posts. In the case of any one of them dying or emigrating, the post went to the nearest qualified relative. In case such a person was not found suitable or available, then the other incumbents of such appointments had to select one among them who was found suitable for the post. The customary perquisites increased the wages of the employees. The wages consisted generally of grants of land plus houses or money, paddy or *prasāda.* Free food was given to Brahmana and non-Brahmana employees. Invariably, well-to-do people were appointed to key posts like the *śrikāryam, bhandārattar, karanattār,* etc. This would have been one way of curbing petty corruption. The rate of remuneration was not on caste lines, but on the nature of work. For example, a Brahmana accountant received the same wages as the superintendent of temple women—2 shares each. It was seen to that the temple servants who were transferred from their home towns/villages were handsomely compensated with house-sites and free food etc. Apart from the monetary benefits the simple fact that they were assigned to the capital city and attached to the royal shrine which held sway over the entire empire, should have been attractive enough for them to readily agree to the transfer.

The division of labour in the temple seems to have been on rational lines. There seems to be no ambiguity or overlapping in the responsibilities and authority of the various administrative staff nor any overlapping in authority. Rajaraja I appointed the *śrikāryam* officer to the head of the administration in his royal temple. This is contrary to the variety of duties held by *śrikāryam* officers in other temples.

The manner of remuneration was such that the burden of paying them their salaries was not entirely with the temple administration. The watchmen were paid by their respective villages from their tax dues. Others like accountants and treasurers were paid directly by the temple treasury. As shall be seen, the money donated to the temple was invested with various villages and the interest accruing on these investments was used to defray the salaries and other expenses of the temple. The burden of supporting such a large temple did not fall on the people of the empire, or else they would have felt resentment towards the royal undertaking. On the other hand, the royal temple benefited the countryside through judicious investments and by redistributing the wealth of the temple.

Above all, the executive head of the temple being a government appointee kept strict check on the activities of the functionaries; being a government appointee, he saw to it that there was no scope for embezzlement of funds. He was the symbol of royal authority in the temple.

These views are best summed up in this quotation by Nilakanta Sastri,[49] "When we recall the nature and extent of the efforts and sacrifices that must have gone to the construction of this magnificent temple, the number of servants and attendants dependent on it after it came up, the method by which these were recruited from different parts of the Cola kingdom and the precise rules laid down for the regular maintenance of their supply, and the manner in which numerous villages all over the empire were linked up with the daily routine of the temple by having to send supplies to it on account of lands held or as interest on sums borrowed from the temple at various times, when we consider further how all the learning and arts that flourished in the country was impressed into the service of this temple, we cannot fail to observe how the Great Temple came to hold, from its very inception, a prominent place in the polity of the land. The temple was meant to dominate Tanjavur, as Tanjavur dominated the rest of South India, at the time it was, indeed, the masterpiece of Rajaraja's rule."

SECTION II

ECONOMIC REACH OF THE TEMPLE

The economic activities of medieval temples of South India constituted a major role played by the temple as the nucleus of medieval society. The activities included: receiving land grants to the temple (known as *dēvadāna*); money-lending activities undertaken by the temple, which yielded income in the form of interest on deposits; financial investments in the development of agriculture and irrigation which in turn yielded additional revenue for the temple; loans to groups like shepherds which were paid back in the form of ghee, oil or by way of interest to the temple. The land grants made by kings and others yielded revenue necessary for conducting the services in the temple as well as for paying the salaries of temple staff. The cash grants to the temple, again by individuals, groups or kings, were lent out on interest, which augmented the income of the temple. These are some of the ways in which the medieval temple involved the countryside and brought about closer interaction between the temple and the different sections of the society.

Perhaps no other temple of medieval South India could match the wealth of the royal temple of Tanjavur for the range of its economic activities. All the land grants made to this temple were by the king who granted entire villages as *dēvadāna*. The revenue yielded from these grants surpassed that of many other large-sized temples. Cash, mainly from war booty, was lavished on the temple. Gold and cash were granted to the temple by the king and his royal retinue. In this, the royal officers and military officers actively participated to make the Rajarajesvaram the wealthiest temple of its times. Not only was the temple rich in resources, but the manner in which the whole of Colamandalam and much of the empire was brought into the economic orbit of the temple, through land grants spread over Colamandalam and land grants made outside (*puramaṇḍaḷam*) the core area, as well as through the cash investments with the assemblies near Tanjavur, bespeak of the magnitude of its economic activities.

As stated above, land grants to most temples (even to royal ones) comprised of portions of villages; whereas, in the case of the Rajarajesvaram, whole villages were granted. The cash invested or lent on interest was given only to village assemblies or *sabhās*. The cash investments from several other temples were lent out to assemblies, groups or even to individuals. This implied a smaller range of cash transactions in the case of these temples as compared to the high sums lent out to the *sabhās* by the Rajarajesvaram. All these point to the grandeur of operations of the Great Temple.

For purposes of analysing the range and effect of the economic activities of the Rajarajesvaram, this section has been divided into two parts. The first part deals with the land grants made to the temple from Colamandalam. A detailed study is made of these grants and interesting information is gleaned from them. The second part deals with the money lent to the *sabhās*. This standard fiscal activity of temples becomes in the case of the royal temple a major source of income for the temple as well as a means at achieving a level of involvement by various officers, military regiments, etc.

LAND GRANTS IN COLAMANDALAM

Rajaraja made extensive land grants to the temple for its expenses (*nibandaṅgaḷ*).[50] The royal order issued by him in his 29th year gives the details of the assessment of the land revenue or *kānikaḍan* due to the Tanjavur temple. This was made to be engraved on stone. The revenue, which was in the form of grain, was to be measured into the temple treasury/granary by the temple measure (called *Ādavallan-marakkāl*), the standard measure.

Rajaraja is credited with having conducted an extensive land survey over the entire length and breadth of his empire covering Colamandalam, Pandimandalam, Ilamandalam and Tondaimandalam. The measurement was precise to the extent of 54,428,000,000th part of a *vēli*, esp. in respect of wet lands. "In elaboration, classification of land varieties and the nature of tax assessment worked out, the Rajaraja survey stands out as an unparalleled instance of its kind."[51] The honour of this extensive land survey goes to Rajaraja and his Officer-in-Charge of the mammoth operations, Senapati Kuravar Ulagaḷandān (One who measured the world), alias Rajamaharajan.

For the purposes of tax collection, there seems to have been an officer-in-charge of paddy supply[52] (as described in the section on Administration).

Over fifty villages were granted to the Tanjavur temple—almost forty of them from Colamandalam. The total revenue accruing to the temple from the land grants in Colamandalam was approximately 120,381 *kalams* of paddy and 1307 *kāśus*. These inscs. give a variety of useful information. The revenue that was waived in favour of the temple was the *'kānikandan'* or the land revenue of the government. The names of the villages granted, the *nāḍu* and the *valanāḍu* (or district) in which they (the villages) are situated. Besides this, the total area of the village, the lands to be deducted as tax-free plus their area; the areas of the remaining taxable land; and the amount of paddy or money to be paid as tax, are some of the very useful pieces of information that can be known from these inscs. The standard rate of revenue was roughly 100 *kalams* of paddy per *vēli* of land. For the villages which paid their revenue in gold, the rate fluctuated between 5.321 and 9.991 *kaḻañjus* of gold per *vēli.*

The village of Arakkankudi in Tirunaraiyur nāḍu[53] had a taxable area of 6.904 *vēlis.* The revenue was 656.614 *kalams* of paddy. The village of Turaiyur[54] in Kir-Palaru of Pachchirkurram (in Mara *nāḍu*) had a taxable area of 147.739 *vēlis.* The revenue amounted to 14,888.509 *kalams,* a large amount.

Though the nature of the land or its productivity is not mentioned in the Tanjavur inscs., the Gangaikondacolapuram (GKC) inscs. give some useful details. Fourteen villages that were granted to GKC were earlier granted to the Tanjavur temple. A study of these fourteen villages tells us the nature of these particular villages. As shown by Noboru Karashima, a comparative study of the inscs. of Tanjavur and GKC[55] reveals that in the case of wet lands (*nīr-nilam*) and (*irupū-vilayum-nilam*), the rate of assessment was exactly 100 *kalams* per *vēli.* Wet lands yielded two or more crops a year, as the term *irupū-vilayum-nilam* tells us. In those villages with single crop lands (*orupū-vilaiyum-nilam*) or dry lands (*puñjey-nilam*), the rate was less than a hundred.

Village No. 22 in the insc.[56] is an example of wet land. This village, Īngaiyūr in Kīr-Palaṛu of Pachchiṛkūṟṟam (a nāḍu in Rajasraya VN), had an area of 42.782 *vēli* of taxable land. The assessment in paddy was 4278.291 *kalams.* Thus, the rate was exactly 100 *kalams* per *vēli.*

Village No. 20 shows an assessment being made in gold. This village, Kuruvaniyakkuḍi in Tiruvālināḍu (a sub-division of Innambarnāḍu), had a taxable area of 39.671 *vēlis.* The assessment in gold was 304.104 *kaḻañju.* The rate was 7.667, which is less than that of other villages in the list. The reason for this variation in rates is not clear.

The forty villages granted to the Tanjavur Temple, which were distributed in several *nāḍus*, seem to have been deliberately chosen from those localities which had similar agricultural systems and productivity. But for a few exceptions where the assessment was made in gold, the rate of paddy paid fluctuated between 99.2 to 100 *kalams* (with a rare exception of 77.237, in the case of village No. 21).

Almost all the villages that were granted were *vēllān-vagai* villages. None of these villages were *brahmadēyas*. This does not mean that grants were not made from *brahmadēya* lands, though in most cases, the lands thus alienated were compensated by other lands. The village of Paḷaiyanūr,[57] a *brahmadēya* in the possession of the *sabhā* of Singalāntaka CVM, was converted into a *vēllān-vagai* village, the *sabhā* getting other land in exchange. After this conversion to *vēllān-vagai*, Palaiyanur was gifted to the Tiruvalangadu Temple. The difference between this village and other *vēllān-vagai* villages is stated in the following terms: "This *ur* is to be exempted from paying tax (*iṛai*) like other villages (*held*) by *vēllān-vagai*, for every year from the sixth, it is to pay a permanent fixed tax (*ninriṛai*) in cash and kind, as paid before including *padi* and *paḷḷi*." As a *vēllān-vagai* village, Palaiyanur had a permanently settled assessment of tax which was paid to the temple now, instead of to the government. Probably, this was meant to leave the actual cultivators of the land in status quo. As a *dēvadāna* grant, the village had to remit a fixed tax to the temple and not a variable one as was the case with *vēllān-vagai* villages. The state's share was generally dependent directly on the annual yield.

Some interesting grants in the Tanjavur insc. include villages 1 and 2. Palaiyur[58] in Inganāḍu is probably identical with Kaḍuvaiyāru in Nagapattinam taluk. The taxable land measured 125.370 *vēlis* and the assessment was 12,530.759 *kalams*. The donated land included the Jaina temple (*palli*) and the land enjoyed by the Jaina teacher. Similarly, Arappal, in the same *nāḍu*, paid a revenue of 10,745.863 *kalams* from a taxable area of 107.614 *vēlis*. This land included those enjoyed by the Jaina temple and the physician (*maruthuva-ppeṛu*). Yet another case of alienation of the land of Jaina *pallichandam* is Nerkuppar of Tiraimur nāḍu. (More on the alienation of Jaina temple lands in the section on Saivism.)

Most of the villages granted to the Tanjavur Temple had an area of less than 60 *vēlis*. A few were more than 100 *vēlis*.[59] As stated above, the villages seem to have been deliberately chosen from various *nāḍus* in order to yield a uniform rate of revenue. Therefore, there is no set pattern in the net taxable area assigned from each *nāḍu*; only uniformity in the rate of assessment was the criteria.

Venni Kurram in Nittavinoda VN paid its revenue entirely in gold. The six villages from this *nāḍu* contributed more than 537 *kaḷañju* gold. Here, the area of the villages granted was small; thus, it is likely that these villages or lands called *nagarams* belonged to the mercantile community. These villages (Nos. 33-38) are stated to have been incorporated (*ivvūraderina*) into a *nagaram*. Villages Nos. 12 and 40 are also *nagarams*.

In all villages, certain categories of lands were exempted from tax. These were lands used commonly by the villagers, their residential areas, their places of worship, etc. The table giving details of revenue from various nāḍus is given along with the accompanying map on land grants in Colamandalam, at the end of this section.

More than 40 villages were granted to the Tanjavur Temple in the core region of Colamandalam. Through these grants an economic liaison was created between the capital—Tanjavur, and the rest of the empire. Enough revenue was generated to defray the expenses of this massive institution, pay for the various religious services as well as provide remuneration for the large number of temple staff. A careful survey seems to have been undertaken to choose those villages whose rate of assessment was approx. 100 *kalams* per *vēli* —the standard assessment for wet lands. Therefore, calculation of revenue was on a uniform basis. Above all, this study shows that Rajaraja had the royal prerogative to grant any area/village in his empire as his gift to the royal temple.

MONEY LENT TO SABHĀS

The temples of South India acted as banks, in the sense that the gold and cash grants which were deposited in the temple were lent out on interest to individuals or groups, though more often to village assemblies, esp. to sabhās. The standard rate of interest was 12% per annum, which worked out to 1/8 *kaḷañju* per *kaḷañju* of gold. This was the standard rate on the investment from religious endowments.[60] In kind, the standard rate worked out at 1 1/3 *kalams* per *kaḷañju* per annum. The interest payable by the assemblies was utilised towards providing various items for the temple, or for the numerous services in the temple.

The cash deposited with the treasury of the Rajarajesvaram Temple was lent out on interest to various *sabhās*. These *sabhās* belonged to various villages situated around the capital of Tanjavur in different *nāḍus* and *valanāḍus*.

This was a standard fiscal activity of most temples. The *sabhās* borrowed the money/gold for various developmental activities. In the case of most temples, the interest accruing from loans to *sabhās* and other bodies was an important form of investment which promised a steady source of income. This income supplemented the revenue from land grants. However, the investments in cash/gold to many of the temples did not amount to much. Cash/gold was often an endowment made by the members of the royal households or top military or government officers who had vast incomes of their own. Going by this argument, it would seem that royal shrines would receive bigger endowments in cash and gold, as the kings and their retinue would be expected to donate liberally in gold to their own royal temples.

In the case of the Rajarajesvaram at Tanjavur, the king, his queens, his sister, other members of the royal household, top government officers like the *ōlaināyagam* and military officers gave liberally to the temple in the form of cash, ornaments to idols, vessels etc. In fact, the list of endowments in gold, silver and other metals to the various images and to the principal deity forms the content of several, long inscriptions giving minute details of the exact weight in gold and precious stones, etc.

Despite this largesse at the command of the 'Big Temple', it has to be noted that comparatively not much cash/gold was lent out on interest. This could mean three things. Firstly, for the Big Temple, interest on endowments was not the principal source of income. The temple by lending out some of its cash endowments to *sabhās* was only carrying out a normal, recognised fiscal activity of the temple as an institution.

Secondly, the financial administration of the temple was diversified in such a way that it was not dependent entirely on any one source of income. This was done in various ways, for example through land grants. Most of the revenue from land grants was in the form of paddy and other items. Only a few grants paid the revenue in cash or gold. The endowments for lamps were mostly made over to shepherds, who promised to supply the required amount of ghee for the lamps.

Thirdly, by minimising the loans to *sabhās*, the royal temple reduced the role/involvement of local bodies in the matters of the temple.

Despite this, it must be noted that more than 11,000 *kāśus* were given on loans to 27 *sabhās*, distributed within a radius of about 50 kms with Tanjavur as the centre. The interest in kind totalled 1149 *kalams* of paddy per annum; and in cash to 1620 *kāśus* per annum. (This does not give the actual figures as the details from some of the inscs. are missing.)

The donors range from the king's sister Kundavai to Guru Īśānaśiva Pandita. Several military officers, army units, royal ministers and government officers are also among the prominent donors. The records give details like the purpose for which the endowment was made; the village which borrowed the money; the amount of the endowment and the interest in kind and cash.

The first grant mentioned here was made in the 6th year of Rajendra I;[61] the rest belong to the 10th year of his reign.[62] *Sabhā* No. 1 borrowed a large sum of money which was contributed by three parties, who had made endowments for specific purposes. To this, the treasury of the temple supplemented 805 *kāśus*. The job of reallocating funds for different purposes was the responsibility of the finance department of the temple. In this transaction, we see the involvement of religious gurus, royal ministers and military personnel. This record shows how resources were redistributed and invested in the countryside from the military sector. Much of the wealth invested in the royal temple was probably acquired from war loot. Thus, some of this wealth went into the development of the agrarian sector through the medium of the royal temple.

The items for which money was granted show the meticulous manner in which the finance administration was conducted. Money had been granted for such items as the purchase of *champaka* buds, cardamom seeds and *khaskhas*. Among the *nāḍus*, Purangarambainādu in Arumorideva VN received the highest amount of nearly 3394 *kāśus* for its 6 villages. Nenmalināḍu (2 villages) with 1354 *kāśus* and Idaiyāḷanāḍu (2 villages) with 1300 *kāśus* were the other major beneficiaries of loans from the temple.

As seen above, army units and military officers, spiritual preceptors and members of the royal family were all actively involved in making cash grants to the royal temple. Cash grants by army officers and army units alone amounted to more than 5619 *kāśus* (more on the involvement of the army and bureaucracy in subsequent sections). Rajaraja assigned selected military regiments the responsibility of the services to images set up in the temple. Many high level officials, like the *ōlaināyagam* and others, were also obliged to make grants to gain the king's favour. Rajaraja, thus, imaginatively involved them in active participation in the management of the royal temple. Here again, the medium of the royal temple as an institution was used to bring about closer interaction between the king, his top bureaucracy and military officers.

TABLE 1

Sl. No.	Nadu	No. of Villages	Revenue Kalams	Revenue Kaḷañju
1.	Arvalakkurram (Arumoli VN)	2	2,383.801	297.28
2.	Nenmalinadu (Arumoli VN)	6	24,270.838	—
3.	Takkalur Nadu (Arumoli VN)	2	5,051.958	167.662
4.	Inganadu (Arumoli VN)	4	28,530.548	—
5.	Velanadu (Kshatriyasikhamani VN)	1	4,918.927	—
6.	Tirunaraiyur Nadu (Kshatriyasikhamani VN)	2	1,192.488	—
7.	Innambarnadu (Rajendrasimha VN)	2	3,517.478	—
8.	Tiraimurnadu (Uyyakanda VN)	1	3,722.052	—
9.	Tiruvalinadu (Rajendrasimha VN)	2	2,929.000	304.197
10.	Venni Kurram (Nittavinoda VN)	6	—	538.088
11.	Chemburaokkandam (Rajasraya VN)	1	612.166	—
12.	Kalarakkurram (Rajasraya VN)	2	2,626.218	—
13.	Venkongudikkandam (Rajasraya VN)	2	7,099.812	—
14.	Pachchirkurram (Rajasraya VN)	7	32,526.027	—
	Total	40	120,381.313	1,307.165

The table given above identifies the *nāḍus* of Colamandalam from which villages were granted as *dēvadāna*. The revenue yielded by each *nāḍu* is also given. Ref. Inscs. Nos. SII, II, 4, 5.

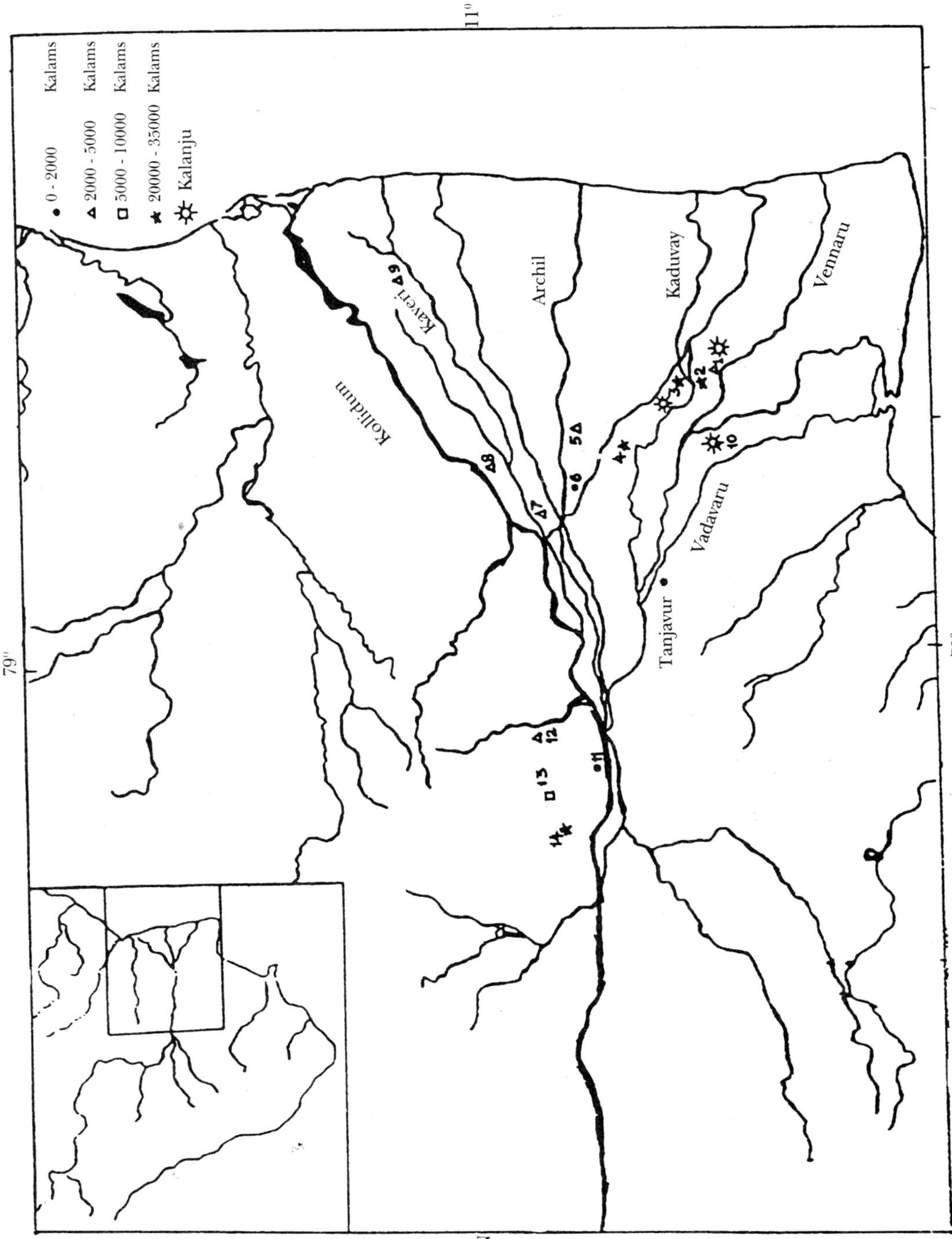

Map I: Land Grants in Colamandalam

A few of these loans by sabhas are analysed in the following table:

TABLE 2

Sl. No.	Sabha	Nadu	Purpose of grant	Donor	Amount Kasu
1.	Nedumanal (Madanamahjari CVM)	Nenmalinadu	a) Purchasing camphor	Guru Isana Siva Pandita	180
			b) Sacred food for image of Kiratarjuna set up by donor	Rajaraj MVN, a minister	13
			c) Sacred food etc. for image of Bikshadevar set up by Queen Lokamadevi	Valangai Parambadaigalilar (Right-Hand Troops)	252
			d) —	Sacred treasury	805
			Total		**1250**
2.	Irumbudal (Manikulachulamani CVM)	Avur Kurram	a) Sacred food	Minister	94
			b) Sacred food	Sirudanattu panimakkal	506
			Total		**600**
3.	Arumorideva (CVM)	Purangarambai Nadu	a) For image of Kalyanasundarar & His consort	Niyayangalilar:	
				i) Keralantaka terinada tirumeykappar	118
				ii) Keralantaka terinda parivarattar	35
				iii) Jananatha terinda partivarattar	5
				iv) Singalantaka terinda parivarattar	1
				v) Anukka-vasal tirumeykappar	8
				vi) Parivara-meykappargal of Tenkarainadu	339
			b) For image of Maha Meru Vitakar	Niyayam Sirudanattu Panimakkal	294
			Total		**800**
4.	Perunangai-mangalam	Venni Kurram	a) Purchase of camphor for perpetual lamp	Tirumandiraolai (headman of Rajakesarinallur of Inganadu)	50
			b) Feeding 240 Sivayogins on 24 festival days	—	100
			c) To buy camphor	Adityan Suryan (Srikaryam of temple)	78
			Total		**228**

SECTION III

THE TEMPLE AND REDISTRIBUTION OF RESOURCES

The redistribution of resources was one of the principal activities of temples of medieval South India. The redistribution of livestock was one such important activity. It ensured a constant supply of milk, curd and ghee to the temples. These were essential for maintaining lamps as well as in the preparation of sacred food and in the performance of rituals. Therefore, all temples—large and small, were consumers of these products. The shepherd community (*manrāḍi* or *iḍaiyar*) were thus closely associated with the institution of the temple from the beginning of the temple movement. Temples entered into agreements with shepherd groups for the constant supply of these items, which were paid for from their cash earnings. In the case of medium or large-sized temples, such expenses amounted to quite a sum. Therefore, it was considered highly pious if endowments were made in cash or kind for the maintenance of lamps. This way, the temples augmented their income for investing in dairy products.

Apart from the cash and land grants that were made to the Tanjavur temple, a number of inscs. give details of the donations of cattle.[63] This was made for the purpose of maintaining lamps in the temple. In most cases, cash was paid to the temple, which in turn paid the amount to the shepherd/ shepherds, who entered into a service contract with the temple and undertook to supply daily a stipulated quantity of ghee for the purpose of lighting different types of lamps. Apart from giving details of several administrative districts of Colamandalam, these inscs. give the names and titles of Cola officials, both military and civilian.

Altogether there are four inscs. which give details of the donations made for lamps. Of these, two, Nos. 63 and 94, were grants for lamps made by Rajaraja himself before his 29th year. Inscs. Nos. 64 and 95 give details of donations made by Rajaraja as well as by others. The king was thus the major donor of endowments for lamps. "Without endowments the king would cease to place himself in an active relationship with the redistributive powers of the deity and thus would fail to acquire the honour constitutive of sovereignty. Without protection, that is, without the authoritative ratification of local regulations by royal edicts (*rāja cācanam*), the king would have abnegated his fundamental duty towards his subjects."[64]

The donations were for maintaining special lamps like *sandhiviḷakku* and *nundaviḷakku.* The total number of lamps, when calculated from these inscs., are 160 in all. For this, the break-up of the cattle donated was 4128 cows, 6924 ewes and 30 she-buffaloes. Out of these, Rajaraja himself granted 2832 cows, 1644 ewes and 30 she-buffaloes (vide inscs. Nos. 63 and 94). From the second group of donations (i.e. Nos. 64 and 95) a total of 1296 cows and 5280 ewes were donated by the king and the others.[65]

The number of cattle assigned to each perpetual lamp was 96 ewes, or 48 cows or 16 buffaloes. Each insc. is a grant for the maintenance of one lamp. For this purpose, either 96 sheep or 48 cows or 16 she-buffaloes, or a combination of sheep and cows was made, i.e. 8 she-buffaloes plus 48 ewes or 2 she-buffaloes and 84 ewes or 4 she-buffaloes plus 72 ewes. Each she-buffalo was equivalent to 6 ewes as far as its milk-yielding capacity was concerned.

Generally, all the cattle from one grant were not given to a single shepherd, but were divided between two or more shepherds or groups/families of shepherds. It is interesting to note that many grants were divided between shepherds who lived in the environs of Tanjavur and others who lived in different districts of Colamandalam, even in far-off Vaḍa-Kōnāḍu. However, most of the cattle was assigned to shepherds in and around Tanjavur itself.

Similarly, a grant for maintaining a single lamp was made up from the number of cattle donated by different persons. For example, in one insc.[66] the total number of 96 ewes was made up thus: a) Rajaraja gave 48 ewes; b) *Perundaram* Uttaranganudaiyan Kon Vidividagan gave 44 ewes; and c) the balance of 4 ewes was taken from the temple treasury from the money which had been deposited for the purchase of cattle. The total number of 96 ewes thus granted was given to three groups of shepherds—one in Tanjavur itself, one in Vinnaneri (a village in Eriyur nāḍu) and another to a third group of shepherds residing in Paruvur in Kunra Kurram.

Thus the administrative officers of the temple painstakingly divided each grant among different groups, in order to ensure that the supply of ghee to a lamp was not concentrated in the hands of any one shepherd or his family. The rationale behind this was probably to ensure continuity in supply, in case any of the shepherds defaulted and failed to reach on time his supply of ghee. However, it would have placed a very heavy burden on the administration of the temple.

In some rare cases, a single shepherd was granted all the cash to purchase cattle required for a lamp. For example, Paṭṭattālaṉ-Achchan-Aḍigaḷ received money for 96 sheep @ 3 sheep per *kāśu* for maintaining 10 twilight lamps (*sandhi vilakku*); he agreed to give one *uḻakku* ghee daily for the 32 *kāśus* borrowed.[67] Another shepherd borrowed 32 *kāśus* at the same rate and agreed to give the same quantity of ghee for 10 twilight lamps.[68]

These shepherds were called upon to deliver a certain quantity of ghee for the lamps into the temple treasury. The shepherds (*iḍaiyar*) had to supply ghee at the daily rate of one *uḻakku* for every lamp, measured by the standard measure—called *'Ādavallān'*. The inscs. do not state clearly whether the shepherds reached their supply of ghee etc. to the temple daily or brought their supply once a week/month. However, an insc. datable to A.D. 1242 from the Sri Varadarajasvami temple[69] states specifically that the shepherds who received the gift of 115 sheep on behalf of the temple, agreed to the condition that ghee and curd should be brought by them daily to the temple kitchen; measured and supplied to the temple.[70] It is however doubtful if the shepherds who resided in far-off areas would have been able to bring in their supplies every day to the temple.

While the *nāḍus* situated in the delta region are beneficiaries of many of the grants to the temple, in the case of lamp grants, the villages mentioned are spread over a greater area all over Colamandalam, though not exactly situated in the fertile tracts of the Kaveri. The fertile delta region yielded the maximum land revenue to the temple, but these areas need not have been ideal pastoral grounds for cattle-rearing. Some of these regions which are mentioned are Rajaraja VN and Vadakōnāḍu.[71]

The accompanying map showing the distribution pattern of the *nāḍus* which received lamp grants is interesting. The distribution has been grouped into 5 distinct geographical clusters. The *nāḍus* of Group I are situated on the fertile river tracts of the Kaveri and the Kollidam. This is a high paddy-yielding region and as such would not have been considered very suitable for cattle-rearing. However, this region is dotted with temple-towns. The temples were the largest consumers of dairy products. Therefore, settlements of shepherds existed in these temple-towns from the earliest times. Group II nāḍus are situated in the deltaic regions, but are located in and around Umbala nāḍu, to the north of Vedaranyam. These areas are between the rivulets of the Kaveri and may not have been very fertile.

Group III *nāḍus* are spread over the regions which constituted Rajaraja VN and Jayasingakulakala VN. Both these regions are not watered by the rivers and would have been ideal dry terrain for cattle-rearing. It is significant that many of these areas are not mentioned or included in the other grants to the temple. Group IV similarly consists of areas called Vaḍakōnāḍu, which were on an elevated dry belt. Group V points to the largest concentration of lamp grants to the shepherds residing around the capital city of Tanjavur.

Most of the lamps were maintained from grants made by the king himself. Maintaining a lamp in a temple was considered to bring great merit to the donor. Therefore, it is hardly surprising that Rajaraja and his family lavished their wealth in lighting the temple with lamps. As already pointed out, inscs. 63 and 94 refer only to grants made by the king. The second group consisted of grants made up jointly by Rajaraja himself and others. Thus, the king was the principal donor of lamps.

Among the individual donors are a group of 14 persons who appear to have made the contribution under special circumstances. Military operations were on at Kōḻi, i.e. Uṛaiyūr (ancient Cola capital). A number of military officers were disgraced by the king for having lost the battle (or quell a riot). They vowed to put up lamps in the temple for fear that the wrath of the king would be brought on them, and their fair names would be besmirched. "The supposed rationale behind the kind of penal provision was that the guilty should be imposed a monetary penalty and the sin be expiated by presenting cattle to the temple. This means that to them a guilt was not only a crime but also a sin."[72] Eight of them have the title *perundaram* prefixed to their names indicating their high status.

Three of these fourteen were arbitrators (*naḍuvirukkai seyda*) and were *Brāhmanas.* One of the donors was the *Senapati,* Kuravan Ulagalandan (alias) Rajaraja Maharajan, who assisted Rajaraja in measuring land and fixing the revenue. This is a fair pointer to the rich emoluments that these military

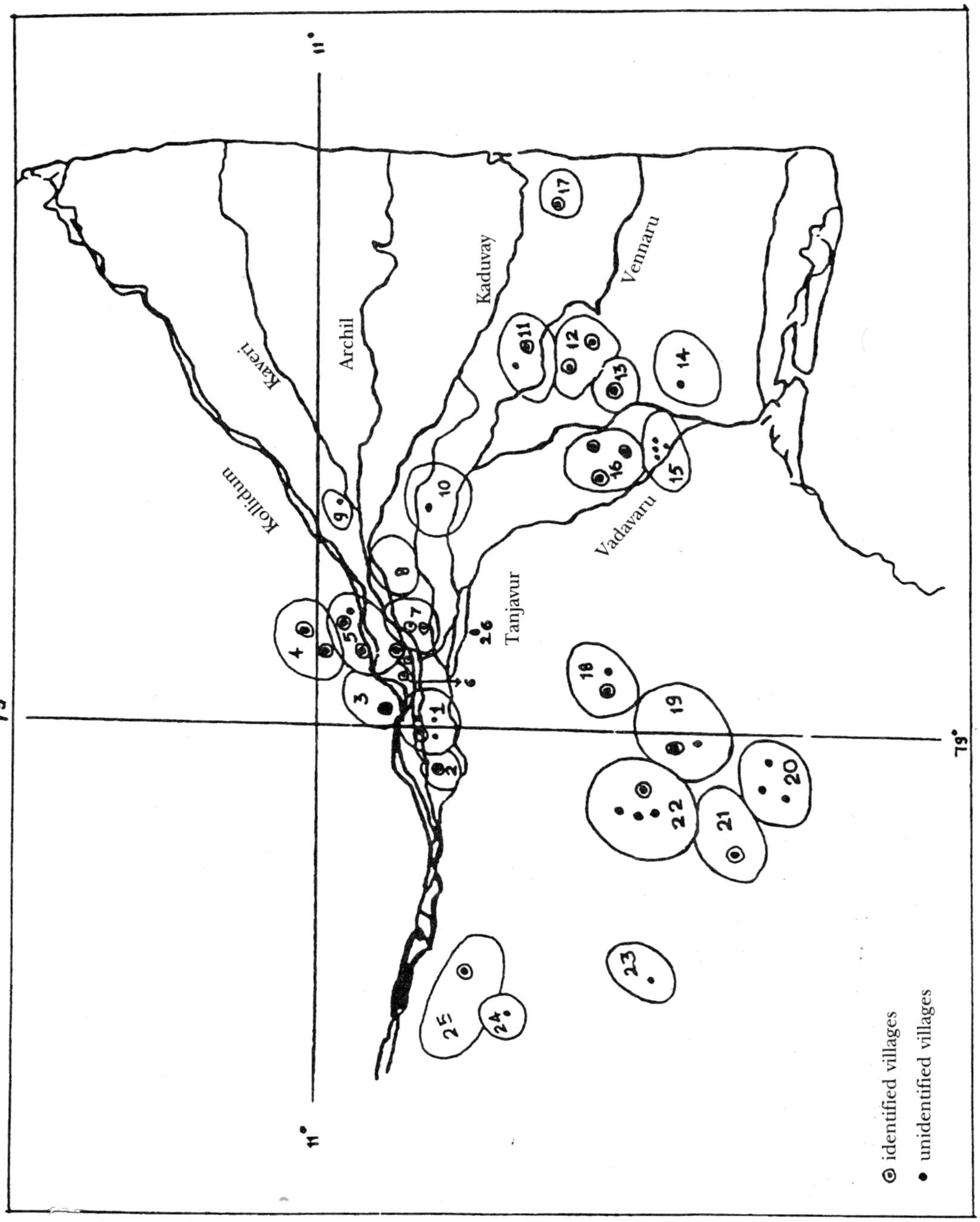

Map II: Distribution of Livestock

TABLE 3

Group	Sl. No.	Nadu	Total No. of Villages	Identified Villages
I	1.	Arkattu Kurram	4	Sandiralegai
	2.	Eyil Nadu	1	Attupalli-Niyamam
	3.	Poygai Nadu	2	Gandaraditya CVM
	4.	Kunra Kurram	2	Paruvur; Iraikkudi
	5.	Mirai Kurram	4	Mirai
	6.	Sri Parantaka CVM	1	Tiruvaiyaru
	7.	Nallur Nadu	3	Perungarai; Rajakesari CVM
	8.	Tirunaraiyur Nadu	-	-
	9.	Manni Nadu	1	Idavai
	10.	Avur Kurram	1	-
II	11.	Mudichchora Nadu	2	Sirrinavur
	12.	Nenmali Nadu	2	Nedumanal; Kottur
	13.	Pambuni Kurram	1	Pambuni
	14.	Purangarambai Nadu	1	-
	15.	Punril Kurram	4	-
	16.	Venni Kurram	3	Puvanur; Kirppundi; Sri-Pudi
	17.	Ala Nadu	1	Sembiyam Madevi CVM
III	18.	Eriyur Nadu	2	Karuvugalvallam
	19.	Kir-Sengili Nadu	2	Mangalanallur
	20.	Panangattu Nadu	3	-
	21.	Vada Siruvay Nadu	1	Valuvamangalam
	22.	Miysengili Nadu	4	Killikudi
IV	23.	Vada Konadu	1	Turaikudi
	24.	Kiliyur Nadu	1	-
	25.	Uraiyur Kurram	1	Rajasraya CVM
V	26.	Tanjavur	-	-

The above table has been prepared on the basis of the *Nadus* which could be identified more or less accurately. The dots represent the villages in the respective nadus. Ref. Inscs. Nos. SII, II, 63, 64, 94, 95.

officers received; or perhaps it indicates their share in the loot from wars which must have been quite substantial. In the later Cola period these high officials became all-too powerful with vast land-grants (*māniyams*), and as the Cola empire disintegrated, they succeeded in proclaiming their independence as small-time kings or chieftains.

Thus the top officials of the Cola administration, high-ranking military officers, royal secretaries, *śrikāryam* officers, arbitrators were wealthy enough to make considerable grants to the Tanjavur temple. This is an example of the way in which the high government officers were involved actively in the affairs of the royal temple. They became participants in this great royal undertaking and were bound to the royal temple by their pious acts (voluntary or otherwise).

Grants were made by individuals on a voluntary basis for acquiring merit. Among them were:[73]

TABLE 4

No.	Individual's Name	Belonged To	Title	or Occupation
1.	Adityan Suryan	Poygainādu	Headman	Srikaryam of temple
2.	Karayileduttapadam	Rajakesarinallur	Headman	Royal Secretary Tirumandira Olai
3.	Sembangudaiyan Amudan Tevan	Sembangudi (Avur Kurram)	Perundaram	Virupparaiyan
4.	Irayiravan	Araisur (Pambuni Kurram)	Perundaram	Pallavarayar
5.	Rajaraja Vanakovaraiyar	—	Perundaram	—
6.	Pudi Sattan	Midur	Headman	—
7.	Namban Kuttadi	—	Perundaram	Jayangonda-Sola Brahmamaharajan
8.	Tirumalai Vengadan	Vayalur	Headman and Perundaram	—
9.	Kon Surri	—	Perundaram	Arumori-Pallavaraiyan
10.	Nittavinoda Maharaja	—	Perundaram	—
11.	Savur Paranjodi	Tanjavur suburb	Superintendent of temple women	—
12.	Achchan Konurkkadan	Tanjavur suburb	—	Merchant
13.	Isanasiva Pandita	—	Guru of King	Chief priest of Rajarajesvaram

The following groups of men are also among the donors.

(a) Udaiyan-Sri-Rajarajadevar-Mummadi-Sola-terinda-parivarattar;

(b) Jananatha terinda-parivarattar;

(c) Palavagai-parampadaigalillar. These were royal retinues.

REDISTRIBUTION OF LIVESTOCK—SPENCER'S VIEWS

This brings us to the interesting inference of George Spencer—that of redistribution of livestock through grants to the temple.[74] In his article, Spencer has described the Hindu temple as a complex, multifunctional institution. Temples are the foci in the networks of social communications and important links in the relatively unstructured systems of political control and influence. The interaction between the temple and society was two-way. The temples performed a variety of activities for the local community, which in turn provided support for the temples' daily activities by donations, payment of interest in cash, etc. The *sabhās* of villages were entrusted with gold deposits of the temples for the payment of interest in the form of provision for rituals, etc. A reciprocal outflow of resources for investment was thus established.

In the case of cattle, the temple assigned donations in livestock to the care of shepherds. This was an *investment* by the temple authorities in the prosperity of the agrarian or pastoral community. The recipients were placed in a service relationship with the temple. By giving cash for the purchase of cattle to the shepherds, the temple invested in the upliftment of the different sections of society. The shepherds who benefited thus from the investment, had the responsibility of providing ghee to the temple (one *uḻakku*). This was the interest upon the shepherds' use of the livestock. The importance to the temple was not so much in the physical possession and disposition of the cattle as in securing certain kinds of daily services to the temple.

"The intention of the donor in donating different categories of the cattle was not merely to supply ghee or curd but also to foster and cultivate the cattle population, which was necessary for the prosperity of the rural economy. The temple as the largest consumer of milk and ghee encouraged cattle-rearing and dairy-farming by having a large contingent of cowherds or manradis to protect the cattle."[75] Enough cattle was given to each group of shepherds, so that the number of cattle multiplied sufficiently in order to sustain the rate of interest in the form of ghee to the temple. Raman has shown how the Varadaraja Temple in Kanci had played a key role in the redistribution of land and livestock and how it contributed to greater agricultural and pastoral activities in that area.

The role of redistribution that the temple undertook, enabled men, money and livestock to be redistributed to ensure higher productivity, greater development and higher remuneration for the community as a whole. This was achieved in several ways. Firstly, by transferring men and women of certain qualifications from far-off areas of Colamandalam to the temple of Tanjavur, the government ensured that they were well-compensated for and remunerated by way of house-sites, money and paddy. Secondly, by investing in cash endowments with the *sabhās,* the temple not only ensured a constant flow of interest on its invesments, but aided in the development of the *brahmadēyas* and their environs. Thirdly, by giving cattle (or cash for the purchase of cattle) to shepherds spread over a vast area, the temple not only ensured a constant flow of interest in the form of ghee, but bound the shepherds to the temple in a service relationship and brought about development of the community. In these different ways, the temple played a crucial role in uplifting and developing the core region of Colamandalam.

This insc. throws light on another interesting feature—the temple served as a channel for the redistribution of funds from the military sector to the agrarian sector. Spencer highlights the temple's role as a major connecting link between the imperial activities of a small military elite on one hand and the agricultural sector of society which it served on the other. The insc. of the Tanjavur temple "reveals that vital economic resources, contributed by the king and other individuals to provide endowments, passed through the temple to various villages in return for the payment of interest or the performance of specified perpetual services for the temple. The flow of taxes and military manpower from the countryside to the royal court was partially counter-balanced by a reverse flow into certain villages of money, livestock and other goods, obtained in part from carrying out plundering expedition into 'enemy' territory. In this way, the remarkable temple at Tanjavur served not only as a means of redistributing resources, but also as a means of binding together court and countryside in politico-economic symbiosis."[76]

Insc. No. 95[77] details the grants of several military officers who were afraid of being disgraced for their part in the *Kōḷ̤i* debacle—all of whom bear the title of *Perundaram.* The military officers who donated lamps for atoning their role in the Kōḷ̤i incident have given almost 800 ewes in all. The donation of the other military officers and military units amounts to almost 512 *kāśus* (figures not complete due to certain inscs. being obliterated). The ancient idea of serving punishment for wrong-doing through pious acts like maintaining lamps in temples seems to be behind the act of penance by the disgraced officers.

This insc. which gives details of donations for lamps is just one aspect of the manner in which the military was involved in the affairs of the temple. This also shows how the booty acquired through wars[78] was redistributed in the countryside (agricultural sector) and how the temple acted as a conduit in this redistributive process. The manner in which the Cola kings brought the entire community together by involving them through the temple is clear.

Quite often, big monumental undertakings have been described as wasteful non-productive expenditure (of which many a medieval monarch was guilty). But when the monumental undertaking becomes a hub of activity bringing into its vortex the different sections of society, making them interact with each other economically, socially, culturally and politically, and when it stimulates economic productivity through judicious investments, then it gives an insight into the shrewd sagacity of its builder in creating an institution by which the different components of the community were not only bound to one another. but also through which all-round development was initiated.

SECTION IV

POLITICAL AND TERRITORIAL REACH

Rajaraja made a grant of more than 16 villages outside the core area of Colamandalam to his temple.[79] This grant is of special significance. The villages/lands granted within Colamandalam were carefully chosen for their rate of assessment (i.e. 100 *kalams* per *vēli*) and the revenue from these 40 villages formed a major portion of the income of the royal temple.[80] The villages that were granted from outside the region of Colamandalam were chosen, not so much for their yield in paddy or gold (i.e. not for the revenue), as for the significance of their geographical locations. These villages chosen with care were located in the kingdoms annexed by Rajaraja in the course of his conquests. This grant shows that "the conquest of those provinces claimed for Rajarajadeva in his numerous Tamil inscriptions was not a mere victorious inroad, but a more or less permanent occupation of them."[81]

The Cola kings took on titles which spoke of their conquests, for example Parantaka I took the title *Madiraiyum Īlamum konda Kōp-parakēsarivarman* i.e. the Parakesari who took Madurai and Ilam (Sri Lanka).[82] Rajaraja introduced an innovation in his *praśastis* by giving a chronological account of the various conquests and other achievements of his career, which have been invaluable for the reconstruction of Cola history. According to his *praśastis*, the first major conquest of Rajaraja was over the Cheras. He destroyed the Chera fleet at Kandalur Salai. He also defeated the Pandya king and annexed his kingdom. Territories known as Sitpulināḍu and Pakkināḍu (vide his 6th year insc. of Kancipuram)[83] were then added to the empire. Next, he conquered Vengi, Gangapadi, Tadigaipadi, Nolambapadi and parts of Andhra Pradesh. The land of the Rashtrakutas called Iraṭṭaipaḍi-ēḻarai-laksham (Rattapadi—750,000) was conquered, as was the kingdom of Kalinga. Rajaraja invaded Īḻam (N. Sri Lanka) and annexed it. Thus, Rajaraja's empire occupied south peninsular India, from the basin of the Tungabhadra in the North and Mahendragiri (Mahendra mountains in Orissa) in the North-East to Sri Lanka in the South.

TABLE 5

Old Name	Region	New Name
Colanāḍu	Core area of Tanjavur and Trichirapalli and Kaveri Delta	Colamandalam
Tondainādu	Pallava country Kanci and environs	Jayangondasolamandalam
Pandināḍu	Pandya country with Madurai as capital	Rajarajamandalam
Nulambapadi	Land of the Nolambas Karnataka and Andhra	Nigarilicolapadi
Ilam	Northern Sri Lanka	Mummudicolamandalam
Gangapadi	Land of the Gangas Mysore dist.	Mudikondacolamandalam
Tadigaipadi	Tadigaivali	Vikramacolamandalam

Much of the details regarding the 16 odd villages have been lost. Despite this, we still find information which is interesting and useful. The villages of Colamandalam paid their revenue mainly in kind. Outside the Cola core region, the revenue payable to the temple was partly in kind and partly in cash or gold. Many of these villages yielded a high revenue in both paddy and gold. However, minute details of measurement, as found in the grants in Colamandalam, are omitted. This is a point to be noted.

The empire was divided into several provinces or mandalams and each mandalam was named after Rajaraja. Rajendra changed or added some provinces of his own.

TONDAI NĀḌU

Tondai nāḍu alias Jayangondasolamandalam had already been annexed to the empire by Aditya I, viz. his title 'Toṇḍai-nāḍu-paavina chōḻan', the Cola who overran the Tondai (Pallava) country.[84] In Tondai nāḍu, the village of

Pērayūr was granted. This village in the Pērayūrnāḍu is a subdivision of Ōyma nāḍu. Ōyma nāḍu is an ancient territorial designation in early Tamil literature. It is identified with modern day Tindivanam in South Arcot dist. The grant states that the previous owners were replaced, and the ryots were removed. The revenue paid as tax by this village included *kārānmai* and *mīyātchi.* These generally refer to the ownership and cultivating rights. The text is not clear and does not furnish more information. Revenue in the form of gold was also paid and amounted to 109 *kalañju,* 9 *manjāḍi.*

MYSORE AREA

A 6th year insc. of Rajaraja is found in the Mysore country.[85] Therefore, he should have annexed the land of the Gangas quite early in his reign. There are two grants in Gangapadi. The first is the village of Alūr in Padināḍu. This Alūr is Alūr in Chamarajanagar taluk; and Padināḍu is in Mysore dist. Here too, the previous owners were replaced. This village paid 500 *kaḻañju* of gold as tax, which also included *kārānmai* and *mīyātchi.* In another grant from Gangapadi (the village name is lost) the previous owners were replaced. The revenue paid as tax was 500 *kalañju* of gold.

PANDYA COUNTRY

The conquest of the Pandyas followed or preceded his campaign against the Cheras. A record of his 20th year[86] mentions that Rajaraja 'destroyed the town of Madurai...' He subjugated the Pandyas and converted Pandināḍu into a new province—Rajaraja-mandalam. The crown prince was generally assigned the governorship of this important province.

Pandinadu has one grant—the village being Anḍakuḍi in Perumbur-nāḍu. Here too, the previous owners were replaced. The revenue paid as tax included *irai-kaḍan, ura-vukōl-nilan kāśu, kātchi-eṟudu-kāśu, ūrkkarañju kāśu,* together with *kārānmai, mīyātchi* and *paravirai* which constituted the portion (Vagai) of cultivators (*Vēllan*). This amounted to 123 *kalams.* Revenue in gold amounted to 284 *kāśus.* The first term *irai-kaḍan* seems to be a tax payable directly to the king. *Ūrkkarañju* is probably a due payable by the residents of the *ūr* and implies that a *kalañju* was collected as tax.[87] Most of the instances of this tax appear in the exemption granted on lands of *dēvadāna* category.

ANDHRA-KARNATAKA

Nulambapāḍi alias Nigariḻisōlapāḍi has two grants. The campaign against the Nolambas and the Gangas is first mentioned in the 8th and 9th years of his reign. Nulambapadi (the Nolambas were subordinate to the Gangas) included, even in the 10th c. A.D., the dists. of Tumkur and Citaldurg, much of Bangalore, Kolar and Bellary dists. and even parts of Salem and N. Arcot. Both the granted villages were in Parivaināḍu and are called Kaśavūr and Kūdalūr. The two are classified as *dēvadāna* and *brahmadēya.* Kasavur paid a revenue of 9000 *kalams* of paddy, while Kūdalūr paid 12,843 *kalams.* Both the revenue amounts are quite high, even by Colamandalam standards. Parivaināḍu owes its name to the Bana capital—Parivai, which could be identified with Parigi in Anantapur dist. Nulambapadi extended into modern Anantapur dist.[88]

KERALA

Pudukkōḍu village of Vellappanāḍu is the grant in Malaināḍu (Kerala). Further information from this grant is missing, except that here too the previous owners were replaced. From the 4th year of his reign, the phrase *Kanḍalūr-Śālaik-kalamarutta* precedes the name of the king in his inscs.[89] This would refer to his expedition against the Chera king, Bhaskara Ravi Varman Tiruvadi. It is generally believed that Rajaraja led two expeditions to the Chera country—one by sea, during which he destroyed the fort of Viḻijnam (on the West Coast) and captured Salai of Poraiyan (the Cheras). The Salai of Poraiyan means Kanḍalūr-Śālai of the Cheras and is between Kanyakumari and Trivandrum on the West Coast. A later insc.[90] refers to his conquest of the Cheras and the Pandyas in the Malai-nāḍu (mountain country). This is also referred to in the Tiruvalangadu Plates, where he is said to have conquered the country created by Parasurama which was "matchless and inaccessible on account of the mountains and the ocean."[91] According to these inscs. Malai-nāḍu is identical with the Chera country (the area around Trivandrum).

SRI LANKA

Īḻam (Ceylon) was among the earliest conquests of Rajaraja (993 A.D.).[92] In his 29th year (1014 A.D.), he made a grant of several villages in Īḻam to his temple, Rajarajesvaram.[93] Rajaraja made himself master of Northern Lanka and made it a province (*manḍalam*) under the name of Mummudi-Sola-Mandalam. Rajaraja ransacked Anuradhapura, the capital of Ceylon and created a new capital at Polonnaruva, which was renamed as Jananatha-mangalam (after one of the names of the king). However, the lands assigned to the Rajarajesvaram belonged to Northern Sri Lanka in Mummudi-Sola-Mandalam. An officer from the Cola country, by name Talikumaran, built a temple called Rajarajesvara at Mahatittha (Mantota), which was named as Rajarajapura.[94] This place is situated in the north-west region of Sri Lanka, south of the Jaffna peninsula.

Five villages were granted to the temple from Īḷam. Three of them were in Mappiśumbu-Koṭṭiyāram alias Rajaraja Valanāḍu. They yielded revenues of 3164, 117 and 183 *kalams* of paddy respectively. The revenues in cash or gold from the first two villages were 12 and 22 *kalañju* resp. They also had to send as revenue oil for burning of the lamps in the Big Temple at the rate of 2,3 and 4 *kalams* resp. In the grants relating to Īḷam, no mention is made of previous owners being replaced. Here obviously, the conditions were different as compared to the mainland. The revenue terms are also not clear.

PREVIOUS OWNERS REPLACED

It is significant to note that in many of the areas the previous owners were replaced. It is not stated by whom. It is likely, though, that in order to ensure a continuous flow of revenue from the granted villages to the temple, the ownership rights of these villages could have been handed over to groups who owned their loyalty to the Cola power. Or more likely, they could have been handed over to military camps. The army seems to have been spread over the country in local garrisons and cantonments called *kaḍagams.*

The destruction of temples, of which Rajendra I is accused in a Calukya insc.,[95] was no doubt due in part to religious differences. Rajendra was a Saiva and the temples in the Calukyan country which he destroyed, were richly endowed Jaina bastis. The villages in Nulambapadi (Nigarili Sola padi) which were granted to the Tanjavur temple were originally *dēvadāna* and *brahmadēya* villages. Being a Saiva, it is unlikely that Rajaraja or his son, Rajendra, would have alienated lands belonging to Saiva temples. Apart from Jaina *paḷḷis* which were converted to *dēvadāna* lands for the royal temple, these could be instances of Vaisnava temple lands being converted to grants for the Siva temple at Tanjavur.

In the region of Īḷam (Northern Sri Lanka), the conditions were quite different. After his conquest of this country, Rajaraja stationed a unit of his army there, probably entrusted with the task of collecting and despatching to Tanjavur the revenue dues, both in cash (gold) and in kind. However, the grants in these villages do not state that the previous owners were replaced. Thus, this aspect was left undisturbed.

Among the revenue terms used are *kārānmai* and *mīyātchi*. In the grants it is explicitly stated that the revenue paid as tax included these two items. These generally refer to the ownership and cultivating rights. It could be interpreted as the previous owners being replaced and the ownership and cultivating rights being transferred to the temple. However, it seems that the temple did not directly cultivate the lands (for practical reasons), and must have handed them over to other parties, who paid as revenue a tax on ownership and cultivating rights. In several cases, the lands thus alienated in favour of the temple were handed back to the previous owners by the temple concerned, on the payment of the above-mentioned taxes.

An interesting observation is made by Karashima in his study of the two villages, Īśānamangalam (a *brahmadēya*) and Allūr (a non-*brahmadēya*), in Trichy dist.[96] From the records on Allur, Karashima establishes the premise that in a non-*brahmadēya* village the *ūr* members were themselves the cultivators. In insc. No. 692, the phrase *kuḍinīkka* occurs, which means that the previous owners were not evicted. Another phrase in the insc. is *ūrē-uḻudukoṇdu*, which means that the *ūr* itself should cultivate the land. Therefore, it is evident from this record that the land was cultivated by the *ūr* members and that the *ūr* members held most of the land in Allur and were, in all probability, the cultivators.

Another record in his argument mentions the phrase *kuḍinīkki*, which means that the previous cultivators should be evicted. The land was obtained from the people of the *ūr* and the previous cultivators, who were evicted, were members of the *ūr* themselves. It states that the temple priests should cultivate the land. However (says Karashima), the priests themselves do not usually cultivate and therefore, the land might have been cultivated by agricultural labourers (other than temple servants). From an analysis of these inscs. Karashima concludes that the land donated to the temple was not cultivated by the *ūr* members themselves, who had been owners of the land. Though there is no evidence in the inscs., lands given as *kāni* to persons for their services were also presumably cultivated by people other than the *ūr* members. This shows the existence of a class of agricultural labourers, who were not members of the *ūr*.

This is an interesting interpretation of the phrase 'the previous owners should be replaced'. However, such a phrase is used only with reference to the land grants to the Tanjavur Temple made outside Colamandalam. No such condition is mentioned in those grants which came within the region of Colamandalam.

These 16 villages outside Colamandalam are of great importance. They show the geographical reach of the royal temple. The influence of the temple covered a vast area of more than 900 kms from north to south. It is obvious that these villages were not granted for their yield in revenue. The grants are a symbolic representation of Cola imperial power. This might be one of the reasons why only a few villages were granted in each province. They are more in the nature of a token demonstration of imperial authority. It would have been easy to grant more villages, but difficult to implement the conditions in the grant. Revenue collection from such far-off places as Anantapur, which is almost 750 kms away from Tanjavur, would have posed practical difficulties. Therefore, only a few token grants were made from each region.

By converting these villages into *dēvadāna* of the royal temple, Rajaraja tried to extend the religious hold of the temple over the conquered areas. Even if the hold of the Cola power on these regions loosened in course of time, the religious bond with the capital city of Tanjavur through the royal temple would have continued. The Siva temples that Rajaraja and his successors built in these conquered regions were modelled, in form and content, after the royal temple of Rajarajesvaram. The administration of these temples and the *brahmadēyas* established in far-off regions (as in the new regions called Jananathamangalam in Sri Lanka) were very similar to those functioning in the core region of Colamandalam. The Cola hold over Sri Lanka disintegrated after almost a century, but the institutions established and the communities introduced here by the Colas continued for long. Thus, a cultural colonisation of sorts was achieved by the Cola conquests. These grants, therefore, give ample evidence of Rajaraja establishing Cola hegemony over the conquered territories through the medium of the royal temple. The institution of the royal temple was used cleverly to extend and establish political control over the conquered kingdoms.

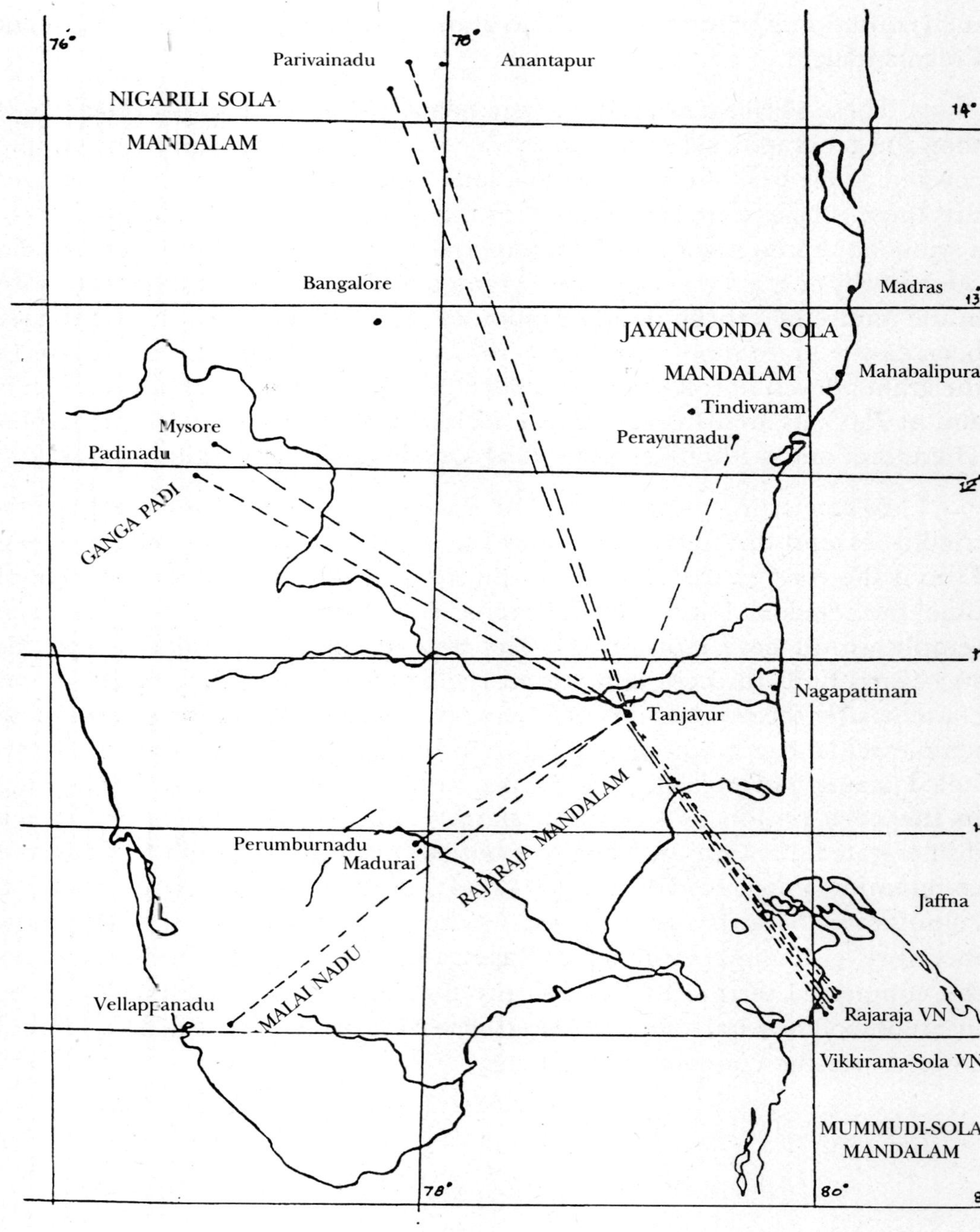

Map III: Territorial Reach of Royal Temple

TABLE 6

Sl. No.	Nadu	Mandalam Name	Villages	Revenue: Kalams	Revenue: Kalanju	Illipai pal
1.	Perayurnadu	Jayangondasola-mandalam	a) Perayur	—	110	
2.	Padinadu	Gangapadi	a) Alur	—	500	
3.		Gangapadi	b) —	—	500	
4.	Perumburnadu	Rajarajamandalam	a) Andakudi	123	284	
5.	Parivainadu	Nigarilisolapadi	a) Kasavur	9000	—	
6.	Parivainadu	Nigarilisolapadi	b) Kudalur	12843	—	
7.	Vellappanadu	Malainadu	a) Pudukkodu	—	—	
8.	Mappisumbu-kottiyaram (Rajaraja VN)	Mummudisola-mandalam	a)	3164	12	2 1/2
			b)	117	1/2	3
			c)	183	22	4
9.	Kanakkan-kottiyaram (Vikkirama-sola VN)	Mummudisola-mandalam	a) Masar	458	—	
			b)	—	—	

SECTION V

SOCIAL REACH OF THE TEMPLE THROUGH THE APPOINTMENT OF TEMPLE PERSONNEL

In his 29th year Rajaraja issued orders to the *brahmadēyas* of Colamandalam, Pandi-nadu alias Rajaraja-mandalam and Tondai-nadu alias Jayangonda-solamandalam. The order [97] said that they should supply to the Tanjavur temple qualified people for different jobs. The order states that the *brahmadēyas* mentioned therein should supply to the temple:

a) as temple treasurers, *Brāhmanas* in those *brahmadēyas*, who were rich in land, connections or capital;

b) *Brahmacarins* (mani) as temple servants;

c) Accountants for writing accounts (of the temple).

Another record,[98] also belonging to his 29th year, gives a similar order to the *brahmadēyas* in Colamandalam, for the supply of watchmen (*tirumēyakkāppu*) for the Big Temple. Although the term 'villages' is used in place of the 'members of the assembly' in certain portions of the insc., they are all *brahmadēyas*, as the order is addressed, at the very start, to the 'inhabitants of the *brahmadēyas* in the Colamandalam'.

Yet another significant record[99] deals with the appointment of as many as 400 temple women (*taḷip-pendir*) to the royal temple, from as many as 91 temples in 52 centres. Some important centres contributed several women. The holy city of Tiruvarur sent almost 50 women to the royal temple. As many as eight women were deputed from a single temple. The fact that such a large number of temple women were transferred to the royal temple, shows that the *dēvadāsi* system was an ancient and well-entrenched practice and that many temples irrespective of their size had several dancing girls attached to them. In most cases, the appointment was made hereditary, which ensured a regularity in their supply.

The employees of the temple were called *nivendakkārar* (*nivendam* or *nibhandam* means a share in the income of the temple lands). More than 800 personnel were on the pay-roll of the temple. In all, more than 40 categories of employees have been listed.[100] The total remuneration in kind to the *nivendakkārar* amounted to 18,925 *kalams* of paddy. The remuneration to *taḷichērip-pendugaḷ*, *Tēvaram* reciters and the wages of *nivendakkārar* together was around 54,125 *kalams* of paddy, in addition to cash for their daily needs. Apart from this, arrangement was made for payments to guards, priests and preachers.

The inscs. provide for this income by altering land ownership conditions and the temple's share in the land revenue; besides vesting the rights of collecting the entire *mēlvāram* from *dēvadāna* lands with the temple. To meet this budget, Rajaraja made the following arrangements: a) wealthy *sabhās* in Colamandalam were required to send guards and preachers on their account. Their remuneration was paid into the treasury of the Tanjavur temple by the respective *sabhās*; b) direct appointees were paid from the coffers of the temple. These included the *dēvaraḍiyār* or *talip-penḍir*, *nivendakkārar*, treasurers, accountants and *Brāhmana* servants. The enormous income of the royal temple from the various land grants and cash investments was used to defray the salaries of the direct appointees.

DISTRIBUTION PATTERN

Approximately 4 treasurers, 14 accountants, 3 sub-accountants and 143 watchmen as well as 178 *brahmacārins* were supplied by 147 villages, lying in eight districts, i.e. Kshatriyasikhamani Valanadu (VN), Uyyakonda VN, Arumorideva VN, Keralantaka VN, Pandyakulasani VN, Nittavinoda VN, Rajasraya VN and Rajendrasimha VN. The number of personnel might have been higher, for in the case of some inscs. the details are missing.

One particular village, Sri-Viranarayana Caturvedimangalam (CVM) in Rajendrasimha VN, provided as many as 12 *brahmacārins*, while Sri-Parantaka CVM (in the same Valanadu) provided 4 *brahmacārins*. Both these villages were *taniyūrs*, i.e. independent village units.

Almost all the villages listed in the insc. (on the supply of treasurers, accountants and *brahmacārins*) had to provide watchmen too. The concentration of villages listed is dense in the delta region, where the Kaveri branches into the minor rivers, the Archil, the Kaduvay, the Vennaru etc. This is also the area where the *brahmadēyas* occupy most of the fertile cultivable

TABLE 7[101]

VN	No. of Villages	Watchmen	Treasurers	Brahmacarins	Accountants	Sub-Acctts.
Arumorideva	38	11	1	35	7	-
Kshatriya Sikhamani	14	26	-	11	-	-
Uyyakonda	24	26	-	35	4	4
Rajendra Simha	43	55	-	65	2	4
Rajasraya	3	5	-	1	-	-
Keralantaka	6	5	1	7	-	-
Pandyakulasani	8	4	-	11	-	-
Nittavinoda	11	11	1	13	1	-
Total	**147**	**143**	**3/4**	**178**	**14**	**8**

tracts. Therefore, it is of little surprise that the *brahmadēyas* in the delta region provided more revenue and staff for the Tanjavur temple.

The order for the appointment of *talip-penḍir* encompassed the entire region of Colamandalam. Almost all the temple-towns of Colamandalam were included in this order to supply women for the royal temple. Coastal towns, such as Nagapattinam and Kaverippumppattinam, were connected to the temple through this order on the *talip-penḍir*. The temple-towns in the delta region became associated with the capital city through this order. Temple-towns to the north of Tanjavur, on either side of the Kollidam, were also included. Thus, as in the case of the order on the supply of watchmen and other functionaries, the order on temple women gives us a good idea of the territorial reach of the royal temple and the manner in which these far-off towns and villages had to supply personnel to the royal temple.

We get an idea of the methodology adopted in taking an initial survey. A census of sorts must have been undertaken from these villages and temple-towns on the number of qualified or suitable personnel available in them. The best or the most suitable ones would then have been appointed to the royal temple. Thus, these orders tell us that Rajaraja not only paid meticulous attention to land survey which yielded maximum revenue to the temple; but also conducted a survey of personnel in Colamandalam, so that the best in manpower could be garnered into the service of the temple.

Incidentally, the order on the appointment of *talip-penḍir* confirms the antiquity of several sacred or *bhakti* temples, which find mention in the

Periyapuranam; for example Araneri at Tiruvarur, Tirukkaronam at Nagapattinam, Aiyaru or Tiruvaiyaru etc. That these temples had several *dēvadāsis* or temple women attached to them is evident from this order.

The order on the transfer of personnel, like *talip-peṇḍir* to the Tanjavur temple from other temples of Colamandalam, is significant. As stated above, most of the temples mentioned are *bhakti* temples and the dancing girls would have been attached to their respective temples for generations on a hereditary basis. That these personnel were in the permanent rolls of the concerned temples is obvious. In certain cases, mother and daughter are mentioned together. Rajaraja transferred these *talip-peṇḍir* to his temple, virtually uprooting them from their homes. That he could do so with impunity is eloquent testimony of the near-autocratic authority of the Cola monarch over his subjects. What is even more interesting is that the king could interfere with the resources of *bhakti* temples in his kingdom. Earlier to Rajaraja's time, kings were wary of interfering with non-royal or *bhakti* temples. Rajaraja and his successors could exercise this prerogative and transfer temple personnel *en masse* from the 'sacred' *bhakti* temples to their own royal undertaking. This shows a virtual subjugation of the interests of most temples to those of the royal temples. The insc. does not mention any effort at substituting the transferred personnel with others. This could be an attempt by Rajaraja to exercise the supreme authority of the government over all institutions within the empire. It also shows the near-total eclipse of power and authority of local bodies in comparison to the government's overriding authority. Local bodies had their independence they were usually accustomed to; but the Cola government, under Rajaraja and his successors, could at any time supersede local authority. This is amply shown in the transfer of the *dēvaraḍiyār* to the royal temple.

RATIONALE

Rajaraja exercised his control over the different communities and the remotest parts of his kingdom, to staff his royal endeavour through the orders on the transfer of temple personnel. His implicit order to the *brahmadēyas* of Colamandalam, to supply staff to his royal temple, brought different parts of his kingdom closer. He did not take recourse to the easiest way out by appointing people close to Tanjavur, his capital; instead, he brought them from far-away centres of his kingdom. What, then, was the rationale behind such an exercise?

Firstly, he wished to bring the different parts of his empire into closer interaction with each other. For this, the medium of the royal temple was used to act as the pivot around which the empire revolved.

Secondly, he exercised total control over the communities in his kingdom, which made it obligatory for them to obey his command and work (or do service) in the royal temple.

Thirdly, the *brahmadēyas* and temple centres became connected to the royal temple in a centripetal movement, i.e. all activities and movement was towards the royal temple, which was the nucleus of the empire.

Fourthly, Rajaraja effectively distributed the burden of remunerating the staff for his temple by making the *brahmadēyas* responsible for the payment of their salaries (as in the case of the watchmen), and did not concentrate everything in the hands of the temple and the royal treasuries.

Fifthly, he assessed the revenue-paying capacity of each *brahmadēya*, and based on this, he placed a requisition on the number of personnel to be supplied and maintained by them. For example, in the case of certain *taniyūrs* like Sri-Viranarayana CVM, the number of watchmen to be supplied was more than one. This was so, because the *taniyūrs* were assessed differently for their revenue.

Sixthly, he gave only the responsibility of remunerating the personnel to the *sabhās* concerned; the ultimate burden of paying them reverted on the government, as the payments were to be made from the tax dues of the *sabhās* and not from their net incomes.

In this royal order, above all, Rajaraja's desire of making the Rajarajesvaram the pivot of his entire kingdom is clearly discernible. Almost every *sabhā* and temple centre was tied to the royal temple through this order for the supply of various staff to the temple. Thus, a service relationship was established between the royal temple and all the regions of his empire. He gave every village importance by being associated to this premier institution of the empire. In a period when communications were not much advanced, he used the medium of the royal temple to act as the communicating factor between all sections of people and all regions of Colamandalam.

A discussion on the significance of the royal order being addressed to *brahmadēyas* is given in the Appendix at the end of Chapter II.

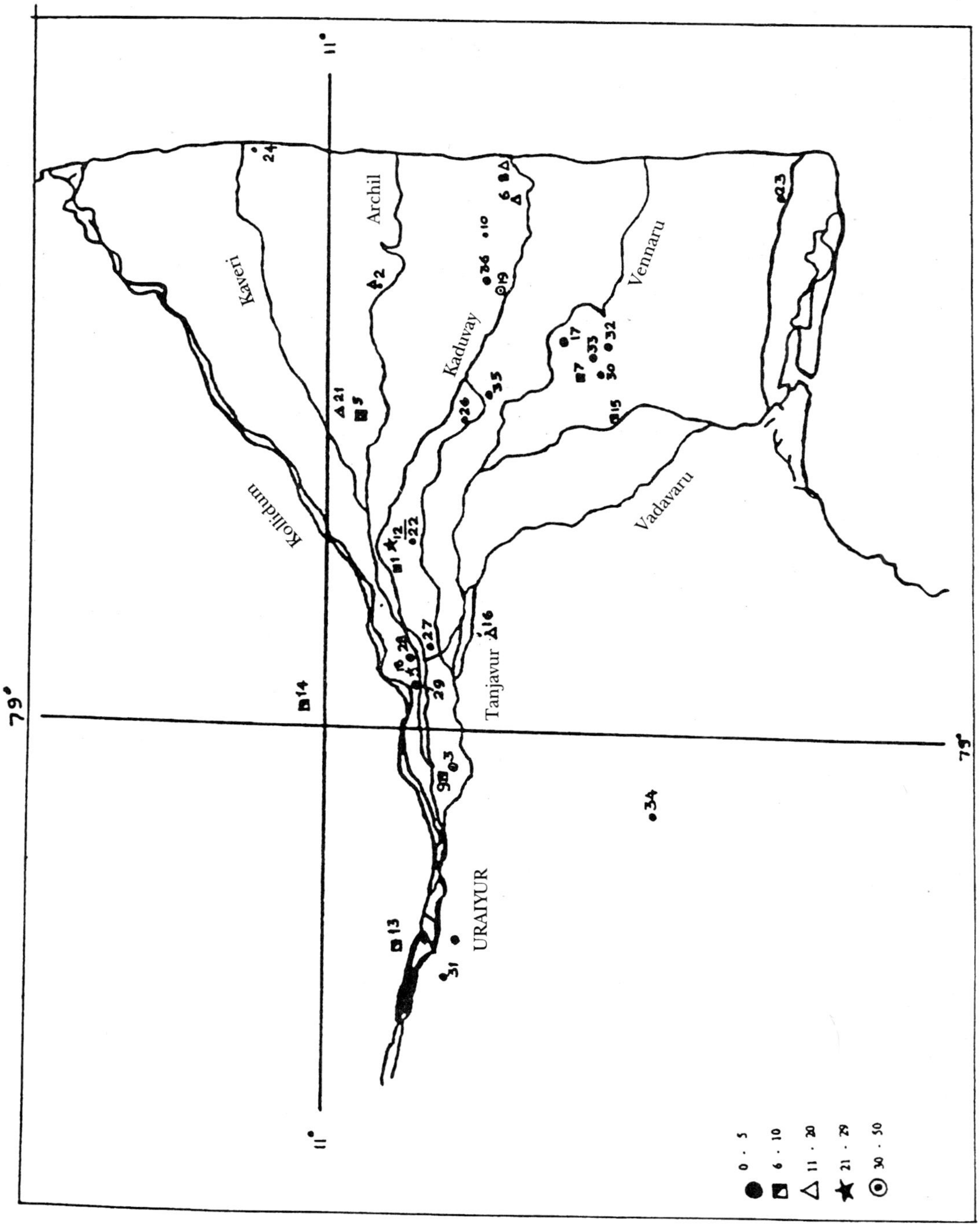

Map IV: Transfer of Talip-Pendir

TABLE 8

Sl. No.	Place Name	No. of Women Transferred
1.	Arapuram	8
2.	Ambar	19
3.	Ayirattali	30
4.	Andali	-
5.	Jananathapuram	8
6.	Kadambur	15
7.	Kottur	6
8.	Nagapattinam	13
9.	Niyamam	9
10.	Nannilan	-
11.	-	
12.	Palaiyaru	23
13.	Pachchil	8
14.	Paluvur	10
15.	Pambuni	6
16.	Tanjavur	17
17.	Tengattur	2
18.	Tiruvaiyaru	24
19.	Tiruvarur	49
20.	-	-
21.	Tiruvidaimarudur	17
22.	Avaninarayanapuram	3
23.	Tirumarakkadur	5
24.	Kaverippumpattinam	-
25.	Pandanallur	-
26.	Tirkkollambudur	1

Sl. No.	**Place Name**	**No. of Women Transferred**
27.	Tiruchchorrutturai	2
28.	Tiruppalanam	1
29.	Tiruneyttanam	2
30.	Tirukorramangalam	1
31.	Vayalur	3
32.	Velur	3
33.	Tiruchattangudi	4
34.	Killigudi	4
35.	Rajakesarinallur	1
36.	Karuppur	1

The above table gives the names of the places which have been identified, more or less accurately. The approximate number of women (*talip-penḍir*) who were transferred to the royal temple from each place is also given.

SECTION VI

THE ROYAL TEMPLE AND SAIVISM

Bhakti, the leading ideology of medieval times, influenced all classes of people. The rulers, in their turn, adopted the prevailing ideology of their subjects. Elaborating on this ideology with the help of temples and through the creation of rituals and endowments, the sovereign assumed the mantle of the premier devotee. The institution of the temple was thus crucial in enhancing the power and influence of both the object of veneration (the temple deity) and the foremost devotee of the god (the king). The kings instituted rituals and festivals and encouraged the chosen faith of the ruling house.[102]

The central actor of the ritual is the principal, i.e., in the case of the South Indian state, the king. The primary goal of the ritual is the generation of prosperity.[103] The king, in the South Indian temple, played the central role of donor of gifts (*dāna*). The act of *dāna* generated overall prosperity by disseminating wealth. This role of the king was performed through the medium of the temple.

IDEOLOGY IN PRE-COLA PERIOD

The Pandyas of the 7th and 8th c. A.D. were committed to the Brahmanical faith in general and were followers of both Saivism and Vaisnavism. The invocatory verses in their copper-plates invoke both the gods, Siva and Visnu. Varaguna I (alias Nedunjadaiyan Parantaka, c. 770 A.D.) called himself Parama Vaisnava and so did his son, Srimaran Srivallabha; but the latter's son, Varaguna II became a devotee of Siva under the influence of his minister, Saint Manikavasagar.[104] So it is seen, in the earlier period there was flexibility in approach. However, after 900 A.D. (perhaps due to the influence from the Cola country), the Pandyas also became followers of Saivism, yet retaining their respect for Vaisnavism.

The same flexibility or non-sectarian outlook is seen amongst the earlier Pallavas. Later some were more devoted to Siva (Rajasimha) and some to

Visnu (Nandivarman Pallava). The former exhibits hostility to Vaisnavism, as attested by his insc. in the Varaha cave in Mamallapuram. The innovation introduced by the Pallavas was in identifying themselves with a chosen deity, especially in the later period. The conceptual equation of the royal family with Siva's family in the period of Rajasimha, the most prolific temple builder among the Pallavas, was realised in the ingenious concept of Somaskanda (Siva, Uma and Baby Skanda), which was given pride of place in the sanctum.[105] He also supported *āgamic* worship in the temples and took on the title of *āgamapriyah.* The subordination of *Vedic* deities to Puranic ones was also complete in the period of the Pallavas.

SAIVISM—THE ROYAL IDEOLOGY OF THE COLAS

The Colas of the Vijayalaya line made Saivism their predominant ideology and gave royal patronage for the promotion of Saivism. This was done in several ways. They built/renovated existing shrines, especially *bhakti* shrines in stone. Here, preference was given to Siva temples, sometimes at the expense of Vaisnava, Jaina and Buddhist shrines. They adopted titles connected with Saivism. All the large royal undertakings were temples for Siva. Through the adoption and propagation of the cult of *liṅga,* the Colas universalised a new aspect into the worship of Siva. Under the guidance of royal preceptors and *gurus,* the Cola monarchs accepted the Sudha Saiva philosophy. As a natural corollary, *āgamic* worship was emphasised. This is seen in a) temple architecture, b) the iconographic innovations that were introduced, c) the *āgamic* arrangement of deities in the subsidiary shrines or niches, d) the *āgamic* conduct of worship under chosen spiritual functionaries called Śaivācāryas etc. The temple precincts were expanded to incorporate popular deities into the *parivāra* of Siva, especially under the Later Colas. The discovery of the *Tēvaram* hymns, probably under Rajaraja I, led to the *Tiruppadiyam* being institutionalised.[106] Special *pūjās* and festivals were introduced in temples on special occasions and the kings lavished their wealth on the Siva temples built by themselves. At the same time, they succeeded in involving their royal retinue in actively participating in temple activities.

Of the Early Colas, it was Aditya I who is credited with having built innumerable Siva temples on either side of the Kaveri.[107] In actual fact, most of them were existing shrines of brick and mortar, which were rebuilt in stone by the Early Colas. His son raised a shrine over his sepulchre and established a *liṅga* on it. The temples which came up in Aditya's time included the

Nagesvaram at Kumbakonam, Kilaiyur, Lalgudi and the Muvarkoil (built by the Kodumbalur Chief Bhuti Vikrama Kesari). The Saksinatha Temple at Tiruppurambayam was converted into stone by Aditya I and later called Adityesvaram. Parantaka I continued the work of his father, and he and his successors rebuilt in stone several temples which are mentioned in the *Tēvaram.* The temple at Tirunavalur the birth place of Sundarar was built by the eldest son of Parantaka I, Rajaditya and called Rajadityesvaram. The queens of the Cola house also built several temples to Siva. Tiruvakkarai, Tirumudukunram, Arur-Araneri, Tirumanayam, Tirucceyalur, Tiruvenkadu, Tenneri, Tirumangalam etc. were all renovated in stone by Sembiyam Madevi, the queen of Gandaraditya.

Rajaraja built many temples and renovated several others in stone. Some of them were the Jayankondacolisvaram at Sengunram (North Arcot), the Cholendrasimhesvara at Melpadi, the Cholendrasimhesvara at Seramadevi (Tirunelveli Dist.), the Rajarajesvara at Nagercoil (Kanyakumari Dist.), the Rajarajesvara at Cholapura near Vellore and the Rajarajasvami at Sivapuram near Madras. Thus, the Colas after Aditya I built and renovated countless temples to Siva.

ALL ROYAL TEMPLES ONLY FOR SIVA

All the great royal ventures were only for Siva. The royal temples of Rajaraja I and Rajendra I were built in the capital cities of Tanjavur and Gangaikondacolapuram. The royal temple held a position of pre-eminence in the capital *vis-a-vis* other temples in the empire. Such magnificent monuments glorified Siva as the Supreme Lord. Rajaraja's greatest edifice was dedicated to Siva. The Rajarajesvaram was named after himself quite after the fashion of the Pallava kings, like Rajasimha, and the Early Colas like Aditya I. This custom seems to have originated in S-E Asia. The tutelary god of the Cham dynasty appears to have been Bhadrēśvara (a Sivalinga).[108] The fourth century warrior king, Bhadravarman, constructed a wooden temple in honour of this Sivalinga. From this time onwards the kings of Champa formed the name of their national deity by combining the name of the reigning king with 'esvara', i.e. Siva.[109]

Rajaraja made his temple the biggest one of its time, both in size and in reach. The other great temples of the quartet of Cola royal temples were Gangaikondacolisvaram, named after the title assumed by Rajendra I in his capital of the same name; the Airavatesvara or Rajarajesvaram of Rajaraja II at

Darasuram and the Kampaharesvara of Kulottunga III at Tribhuvanam. All these temples glorified Siva and the chosen faith of the Colas, Saivism.

TITLES ADOPTED BY RAJARAJA

Some of the titles that Rajaraja adopted show his ardent devotion to Siva. His name as crown prince was Arumoḻideva. After ascending the throne, he took on the title of Rajaraja. This name was one of the names of Kubera (the god of wealth), who was an ardent devotee of Siva. Another title assumed by him was 'Śivapādaśēkhara', literally meaning 'one who has his head under the foot of Siva'. Both these titles were assumed around the same time, and were perhaps conferred on him by the temple authorities of Chidambaram. These titles are mentioned in an important insc.[110] on the walls of the Tanjavur temple.

Rajaraja's devotion to Siva is further reflected in the naming of the standard measure of paddy. This was a wooden measure or *marakkaḷ*, which was named as '*Ādavallān*'. This was the standard royal measure and was equal to a '*rajakesari*'. A copy of this measure was kept in the temple in the shrine of *Ādvallān* (also called Dakshina-meru-vitankar). *Ādavallān* is one of the names of the god who dances (Nataraja in Chidambaram). Rajaraja introduced this uniform measure throughout his kingdom.

Rajaraja lavished much of his booty from war on the temple. He gifted a golden bugle with two pipes with his name on one of them. When the deity was taken out in procession, the bugle was played.[111] According to the Saiva Siddhanta philosophy, the effacement of 'I' or '*ahamkāra*' was necessary to the realisation of *Śivānbhūti* (Godhead). Rajaraja is said to have been very religious by nature. He was influenced by his grand-aunt, Sembiyam Madevi and by his sister, Kundavai. He lived in the constant company of *Śivabhaktas* and towards the end of his reign he almost lived like a *Śivayōgi*.[112]

CONVERSION OF NON-SAIVA TEMPLES

Although the Colas proclaimed to be patrons of all religions and are credited with the construction and renovation of Jaina and Buddhist *pallis* in Nagapattinam and other places, their chosen god was Siva. The Naganatha temple, Karpardisvara temple at Thiruvalanculi, Tiruvidaimarudur etc. are just a few examples of the ancient Siva temples which received royal patronage from the Colas. While many of the Siva temples of the Palaiyaru-Kudamukku complex show some evidence of Cola patronage, the Vaisnava temples are *nearly* devoid of any royal patronage. While support to Siva temples by the Early Colas seems to have been an expression of religious piety, the same cannot be said for Rajaraja and his successors to the Cola throne. They championed Saivism rather blatantly, often at the expense of Vaisnavism.

This bias towards Saivism at the expense of other faiths is evident from the inscriptions of the Rajarajesvaram. The properties of several temples or *pallis* belonging to the Jainas were given to the Tanjavur temple by Rajaraja. The records which refer to the land grants to the Tanjavur temple made in the 29th year of Rajaraja,[113] give examples of lands belonging to Jaina temples which were thus made over to the Siva Temple of Rajarajesvara. Insc. No. 2 refers to the grant of the village of Palaiyur in Inganadu. The donated land included the Jaina Temple (*paḷḷi*) and the land enjoyed by the Jaina teachers; No. 3 is a grant of the village Arappar of Inganadu and the donated land included the land enjoyed (*nayvalam*) by the Jaina temple and the physician (*maruttuvapperu*). Similarly, in insc. No. 17, the land belonging to the Jaina *paḷḷichandam* is not among the exempted land, which quite often included Brahmanical temples, especially Siva temples. The Tirunagesvaram which can trace its history to the times of the Saiva saints, became important under the Early Colas, who replaced an earlier Jaina settlement around a *palli.* This was patronised by the *perunāttār* (merchants of the big township) of Kumaramartandapuram in Tiraimur nāḍu. There is a reference to their renovation work, dated somewhere towards the end of the 9th c. A.D.[114] The *nagara* of Kumaramartandapuram was associated with the economic activities of Tiruvidaimarudur and the Jaina settlement of Tirunagesvaram. The Naganatha temple,[115] which replaced the Jaina *paḷḷi* of Tirunagesvaram, received land and money from the members of the royal family and their retinue.

During the rule of the Later Colas, the pronounced animosity towards Vaisnavism manifested itself in several ways. The activities of reformists like Ramanuja to widen the social base of Vaisnavism, could be one of the reasons for Saivite ideologists to adopt a hostile attitude to Vaisnavism. This led to the persecution of Vaisnavas of Chidambaram during the rule of Kulottunga II. As rightly observed by Prof. Sastri, "From this period onwards Saivas and Vaisnavas of South India became strangers to that friendly feeling which subsisted between them in an earlier age when they waged a common war against the Bauddhas and the Jainas."[116]

THE CULT OF LIṄGA

While the association and adoption of a popular ideology was important for the legitimation of a dynasty, the introduction and propagation of a new cult further gave it a messianic role. Bhakti Saivism was the ideology chosen by the Colas. This was because Saivism became "a more efficacious instrument of acculturation for acquiring a wider, popular base in the hands of the Saiva *nāyanārs* and subsequently because of Cola royal patronage...developed its propensities systematically. The worship of the *linga* as the royal cult of the Colas was of central importance in this process."[117] Bhakti temples of Siva existed in the Tamil country from ancient times, but only as small shrines. The *Paripāḍal* mentions for the first time the temple milieu. Koccengannan, the Cola king mentioned in the Sangam, is famed for his temple-building activities. Bhakti Saivism was what inspired the Early Colas to build and renovate temples to Siva, their chosen god. Thus, temples were the manifestation of the ideology of *bhakti.*

The cult or the practice of a creed can differ from time to time and from place to place. The royal Saiva cult of the Pallavas was that of the Somaskanda. The cult propagated by the Colas was that of *liṅga* worship. This is not to say that *liṅga* worship was new in Siva temples. In fact, *liṅgas* were in worship from earliest times. *Liṅgas* are referred to as 'Śīsnadēva'[118] in the Rgveda. The Tamil hymnists describe the *liṅga* variously as *Tāṇu, Kampam* and *Taparam.* "The appellation 'Siva' itself meaning 'red' in ancient Tamil, and the *Vedic Skambha-yūpa* symbolism gets consolidated into the aniconic *liṅga* shaft which was indeed a primeval pillar of fire and becomes the ubiquitous representation of Siva in abstract, around which several new philosophical, radical-esoteric manifestations were predicted."[119] A probable reason for the popularisation of *liṅga* worship may have been the prevailing use of columns or upright stones in ancestor worship in South India.[120] The idea of the deity residing in a pillar was a further development. This was worshipped by the early Tamils, who now visualised it as Siva emerging from the *liṅga.* This concept formed the basis of a new iconographical representation of Siva as Lingodbhava. This new concept was also used to show the subordinate status of both Visnu and Brahma to Siva.

The change brought about by the Colas was to make the *liṅga* the *mūla-bhēra* everywhere. That is to say, no iconic form of Siva could be taken into the sanctum; only the aniconic *liṅga* could be the principal deity of Siva temples. This was a marked deviation from Pallava times when the iconic form of Siva could be the principal deity in the sanctum, for example the 'Somaskanda . In earlier times, thus, there seems to have been a flexibility in the interpretation and application of the *āgamas.* But, with the increase in the influence of Saiva *maṭhas* and Saiva philosophies, which propagated Siva in the aniconic form, strict adherence to forms of worship in the sanctum was enforced. In this, the Colas projected themselves as Sudha Saivas, who firmly enforced the Saivagamas, according to which the *liṅga* was the only form of Siva to be worshipped in the sanctum. As a natural corollary, the Colas established *liṅgas* in all Siva temples. The major Cola shrines at Tanjavur and Gangaikondacolapuram emphasised canonical forms of Siva worship with "powerful elements of ancestor worship of the massive *liṅga* and the focus upon the royal house as cult centres through the worship of the dead king at his *paḷḷipaḍai* and samadhi shrine. The massive Sivalinga incorporated both developments symbolically."[121]

In the Rajarajesvaram, a huge *liṅga* of massive height and girth was installed. It is an enormous monolithic, plain, cylindrical *liṅga* of 1.66m diameter. It was called Rajarajesvaram Udaiyar. The *liṅga* in the temple at Gangaikondacolapuram is the largest monolithic *liṅga* in the Tamil country.

MAṬHAS AND RELIGIOUS HEADS

One of the important contributions of Rajaraja to Saivism was bringing into the Tamil country votaries of different schools of thought in Saivism. *Maṭhas* and *maṭha* heads played an important role in the propagation of Saivism. Increase in the number of Siva temples led to a multiplication of Saiva *maṭhas.* This, in turn, led to an increase in the movement of monks and created countrywide contacts. Rajendra's conquest of the North inspired him to import Śaivācāryas, especially of the Golaki *maṭha,* from the Andhra and Kannada country. By the 10th c. A.D. Saiva *maṭhas* had been established in S. Arcot, N. Arcot, Tanjavur, Trichirapalli, Pudukottai and Ramanathapuram districts. The preceptors of the Golaki *maṭha* were active for a long period in the Tamil country. They propagated Golaki *dharma,* which was Siddhanta philosophy. *Māhēśvaras* of this sect belonging to different temples played an important role in temple administration.[122]

Maṭhas played an important role in imparting religious and moral education. They were the resting places for devotees and centres of charities. Saiva *maṭhas* were connected with the affairs of temples. Initially, *maṭhas* were residences of saints in temples and propagated the *bhakti* ideology. They were indistinguishable from temples in the beginning. By the 9th-10th c. A.D. *maṭhas* had their own identity and helped in supervising the temples to which they were attached. Growth of the *maṭhas* was related to the growth of temples into complex institutions. During the Cola period, there was an increase in the rituals and festivals in temples. This, in turn, led to an increase in the number and importance of *maṭhas*. *Maṭhas* had their own organisational set-up and resources and became independent institutions.[123] The most important role of the *maṭhas* and the *maṭha* heads was the supervision of temple rituals. The pontiffs were well-versed in *Śaivāgamas* and *Siddhāntas*. The worship in the temples and the festivals were supervised by the pontiffs. By the 13th c. A.D. *maṭhas* became as important as temples and even had their own deities.

The influence of these *gurus* on the Cola kings was immense. It was under their guidance and direction that Rajaraja and the other Cola monarchs after him constructed temples, adhering strictly to *āgamic* rules. The *pūjās* were conducted according to the *āgamas*. The *śaivācāryas* and *māhēśvaras*, who were the authorities on *āgamas*, constituted the administrative body of several temples.[124]

The pontiffs of the Golaki *maṭha* were the royal priests of the Colas. They saw to it that the worship in the temples was conducted in strict accordance with the *āgamas*. Rajaraja's *guru*, Īśānaśiva, authored a work called Siddhānta-sāram; Somēśvara wrote the Siddhānta Ratnakara. He was well-versed in Śaiva-darṣana and the eighteen *vidyas*. Trilochana Śaivācārya wrote the Siddhanta-saravali. In this work,[125] it is mentioned that Rajendra I brought from North India Śaivācāryas and colonised them in the Tamil country, and refers to the Śaivācārya as 'our master' (*nam uḍaiyār*). Gradually, the pontificate came to be known as Svāmidēvar and continued right up to the times of the last ruler, Rajendra III.

The influence of these Svāmidēvars was immense. According to a record from Tirukadavur,[126] the Svāmidēvar revoked the king's order appointing two priests to the temple while appointing two others in their place. The appointment was approved by the king. However, kings also exercised their power over the *maṭhas*. In a case of misappropriation of funds by a pontiff in Govindaputtur (Trichi Dist.), the king ordered his property to be confiscated and attached to the temple and the pontiff was expelled.[127] Similarly, Rajendra Cola ratified the appointment of Tirukkarrali Nambi as the head of the *maṭha*.[128]

The Sudha Saiva philosophy of the Golaki *gurus* was similar to that of the Saiva Siddhantins. According to this, only total and unequivocal *bhakti* to Siva was called for. Therefore, it would seem 'Uma-Sahita Paramesvara', the principal deity during Pallava days, was rejected. When the Tanjavur temple was built, there was no adjoining shrine for Amman or Parvati in the precincts of the temple. The first adjoining shrine in the Tanjavur temple was that of Ganapati Pillaiyar. Only in the later period were separate shrines to Amman built. It is also important to note that there are very few village deities in the Tanjavur temple. The shrine of the village deities was clearly distinguished from orthodox Brahmanical temples, to which the term 'Srikōyil' was applied. The *maṭha* heads ensured the pure Brahmanical nature of the royal temples.

SAIVA ICONOGRAPHY

During the middle Cola period, Saiva iconography was elaborated and enlarged. New icons were attributed to Rajaraja in the Tanjavur Temple, as for example the image of Kiratarjuna and that of Pichchadevar which were set up by Queen Lokamahadevi.[129] This image agrees with the description of Bhikshatanamurti. Several icons of Siva were set up by different queens of Rajaraja, like the images of Kalyanasundarar, Lingapuranadeva or Lingodbhava, Nataraja, Srikanthamurtigal and Pasupatimurti, etc. The images of Dakshinamurti, Ardhanarisvarar, Chandrasekhara, Ganapati, Subrahmanya, Visnu etc. were set up by the king himself. Thus an entire Siva pantheon was introduced in the royal temples.

Chandesvara was among the Saiva saints who were consecrated by the king.[130] Chandesa was the foremost among the devotees of Siva. All transactions in a Siva temple were usually done in his name. The Chandesvara shrine was very much a part of the original master plan and was built before Rajaraja's conquest of the 12,000 islands. The shrines of Dakshinamurti, Subrahmanya and Amman were of different dates and belong to a later period. The Amman shrine of Ulagamuludaiya Nachchiyar, now called the Brihannayaki, is a Pandya foundation of the 13th c.[131] In the early and middle periods of Cola rule, there were no separate shrines for Amman in Siva temples. In the early Cola period there were instances of metal images of Devi in the main shrines itself and in the Srīvimāna niches.[132] One of the earliest instances of the construction of an Amman shrine is that of Sivakami Amman, known as the temple of Tirukkamakkottam Udaiya Nachchiyar, in the Nataraja temple at Chidambaram. This temple for Amman was built during the period of Kulottunga I and his successors.

Among the mural paintings in the Tanjavur temple is the fine representation of Tripurantaka, where Siva destroys the three Asuras. Siva as Tripurantaka is shown riding a chariot driven by Brahma; the wheels of the chariot are provided by Chandra and Surya; Visnu is his arrow; Agni is its barb and Yama is its feather. Thus, the complete subordination of Visnu, Brahma and other gods to Siva is to be noted in this iconographic representation. Similarly, the representation of Lingodbhava shows the superiority of Siva to Visnu and Brahma. The shaft of fire which represented Siva had no origin and no end; and Visnu as the boar and Brahma as the swan gave up their futile attempts at finding the same. Yet another iconographic innovation of the Cola period was Siva as Sarabhesamurti. When Visnu appeared as Narasimha, the terrible countenance did not subside. Alarmed by this, the *bhaktas* prayed to Siva for help. Siva assumed an anthropomorphic form known as Sarabha, subdued and overcame Visnu as Narasimha. The devotees hailed Siva as Sarabhesamurti. The idea was clear, that of presenting Siva as the subduer of Visnu. There is a beautiful representation of Sarabha in the Darasuram Temple.

These iconographic forms which proclaimed the superiority of Siva were popularised and spread by the Colas through their temple architecture and sculpture. The intention was to create a Saiva pantheon which could equal and outdo the popularity of the Vaisnava *avatāras.*

RAJARAJA AND THE TĒVARAM HYMNS

One of the most significant contributions to Saivism under Rajaraja was the recovery of the *Tēvaram* hymns. The ritual singing of the hymns, known as the *Tiruppadiyam* in temples, is a practice of great antiquity. The singers of these hymns were called '*Tiruppaḍiyam Vinnappam Seyvār*' or '*Pidarar*'. An insc.[133] of Nandivarman III in the Bilvanathesvara Temple at Tiruvallam records the provision made for those who were to sing the *Tiruppadiyam.* This is considered the earliest epigraphical reference to an endowment for singing the *Tēvaram* and belongs to the middle of the 8th c. A.D. A few early Cola references to gifts for the recitation of the *Tēvaram* hymns belong to the reign of Parantaka I.[134]

Rajaraja is credited with recovering the vast and rich treasures of the *Tēvaram* hymns. Nambi Andar Nambi, who is said to have been his contemporary, was persuaded by Rajaraja to reveal the existence of the lost hymns. Nambi revealed that the full set of *Tēvaram* hymns lay in a heap of cadjan leaves in a room in the eastern *prakara* of the Nataraja temple at Chidambaram, under the seal of the hymnists themselves. The *Dīkshitars* of the temple stated that the room could be opened only when the saints themselves were physically present. Rajaraja hit upon a stratagem. He arranged for a festival in honour of the Tamil *nāyanārs*, and their images were placed in front of the room. The seal was broken and the closed room thrown open. Nambi Andar Nambi wrote a redaction of the *Tēvaram* hymns. Chidambaram became known as 'the *kōyil*'—the temple of all Saivite temples in the Tamil land; and Rajaraja, the saviour of the Tamil hymns. He was given the title of *Tirumuṛai Kaṇḍa Coḻan.*[135] Rajaraja deified the Saiva saints by setting up their images in his temple and highlighting their lives. The murals in the temple show the lives of Sundarar, the story of Siruttonda Nambi and the image of Tiruttondar, which led to the canonisation of the saints. This was one of the greatest achievements of Rajaraja for the propagation of Saiva ideology. Not only is he credited with the recovery of the sacred hymns—for which posterity justly glorified him, but he made these saintly followers of Siva objects of worship themselves. The foremost *bhaktas* of the Lord were equally venerated. He built shrines for Chandesa, the supreme *bhakta* of Siva, and he set up icons of the saints and introduced festivals in their honour. He also established a portrait image of himself, thus joining the pantheon of Siva *bhaktas.*

A record belonging to the reign of Rajendra I mentions a *Tēvaranāyakan* or Superintendent of *Tēvaram.*[136] This shows that the singing of these sacred Tamil hymns was not only institutionalised, but that a regular state department was constituted to control and secure its proper performance. Another interesting record of the reign of Kulottunga III from the temple of Nalla-nayanar in Nallur (South Arcot) states that *Tiruvalal* and *Tiruvembavai* of Manikavasagar were sung on special occasions in the temple. *Tiruvembavai* was further divided into 3 sections—mudal, irandam-pattu and kadaikkappu. The right to sing each part was sold to different *devaradiyar.*[137]

Rajaraja appointed 48 *Pidarars*[138] for singing the hymns before Rajarajesvarar, and made liberal provisions for their maintenance as well as that of their successors. The singing of *Tēvaram* hymns by *ōduvārs* was followed in other temples, a practice which has come down to modern times.

THE COLAS AND THE DEVARAJA CULT

An analysis of the concept of 'Deva-Raja' or 'God-King' would help to understand the changes instituted from Rajaraja's times. The aspect of sacral

Hindu kingship received its highest development in S-E Asia, where the Khmer King Jayavarman II (early 9th c.) was considered to be the first to use the 'deva-raja' concept. "Jayavarman II took into his service a Brahmana, Siva Kaivalya, who became the first priest of the new cult, which he established as the official religion. It was that of Deva-Raja, the God-King, a form of Saivism, which centred on the worship of the *liṅga* as the king's personality transmitted to him by Siva, through the medium of his Brahmana chaplain. The prosperity of the kingdom was considered to be bound up with the royal *liṅga*. Its sanctuary was the summit of a temple mountain...which was the centre of the capital...the axis of the universe...From his time onwards for several centuries it was the duty of every Khmer King to raise his temple mountain for the preservation of the royal *liṅga*, which enshrined his sacred ego. Thus arose the great temples which were the glory of the Angkor region."[139] It was probably this idea that influenced the Cola kings after Rajaraja to build their own great temples, incorporating massive *liṅgas*. The Rajarajesvaram remained incomplete. Rajendra I, instead of completing his father's undertaking, built his own great temple at his new capital, Gangaikondacolapuram. Here too, a massive *liṅga* was enshrined.

Although the *dēva-rāja* concept did not realise its full maturity in South India, the emergence of royal tombs or funerary temples is the closest we get to it. In S-E Asia the ashes or the body of the dead king are believed to have been interred and a temple erected over them. As temples, they sheltered a *śivaliṅga* (most commonly called 'Bhadrēśvara').[140]

PAḶḶIPAḌAIS

Paḷḷipaḍais were sepulchral temples raised over the mortal remains of royal persons or saints. Worship in them had *āgamic* sanction. In later periods, kings installed their portrait statues in big temples facing the deity in veneration. We have Krishnadeva Raya and his queens at Tirumalai, Tirumalanayakar in the Meenakshi Temple at Madurai, among many others. However, the practice of building funerary monuments to the kings seems to have been prevalent among the monarchs of the Cola dynasty. We do not get much mention of such practices in later periods. As stated earlier, the Colas retained this distinctly Tamil custom, unlike their predecessors, the Pallavas, who championed a purer Brahmanical form of religion. Portrait statues were installed by the Cola kings at a few places including Sivapura, where the Siva temple is called *īśvara-ālayam* as well as a tomb-atīta-griham.[141] It is such temples which have raised doubts about the Rajarajesvaram too being a *paḷḷipaḍai*.

However, this contention is unfounded as it was built during the lifetime of its builder, Rajaraja, and could not have been a funerary monument.

The management of these *paḷḷipaḍais* and the conduct of worship in them did not differ in any way from other temples. Rajaraja built the Colisvara Temple at Melpadi and called it the Arinjigai-Isvara as the final resting place for Arinjaya, who died at Arrur. This temple was managed by *māhēśvaras*, accountants etc.[142] An insc.[143] belonging to the 9th year of Rajendra I records a grant of ghee by the shepherds of Melpadi to this temple. This grant was made before Lakulīśa Pandita, the head of the *maṭha* connected with the temple (The Pasupata *maṭha* originated from Karohana in Gujarat.)

An unpublished insc.[144] from Darasuram belonging to the reign of its builder, Rajaraja II, states that one Arrurudaiya Kuttan was maintaining accounts of the village of Rajaraja CVM. He was given land grants for doing so. From his grant, he enjoyed half for himself and the other half he paid to the temple. This same person was also appointed as the accountant of 6 *paḷḷipaḍai* temples.[145] The *paḷḷipaḍais* were Rajagambhiraisvaram, Bhuvanamulududaiyal-Isvaram, Tribhuvanamulududaiyal-Isvaram, Elulagamulududaiyal-Isvaram and Ulagadaimukkokkilanadi-Isvaram, probably named after Rajaraja II and the Queens of the Cola family. He received *kāni* grants from each of these six temples.

The difference in perception of the devaraja concept between the Cola kings and the Calukyan and the Northern kings, who claimed divine titles, was the use of the symbol of the *liṅga* as the repositor of royalty. The king was referred to as Rajaraja-udaiyar and the *liṅga* as Rajarajesvara-udaiyar, thereby equating the majestic *liṅga* with the great king. The king demanded veneration to his god (Rajarajesvara) which in turn was converted into veneration for the king himself. This is a deviation from the idea of incarnation (as in the case of the Calukyan kings) and seems to be an influence from the Khmer kings and their concept of *dēva-rāja.*

The personality cult of the king was further emphasised by the recitation and enaction of a drama called 'Raja-Rajesvara-nataka',[146] which described the building of the great temple. Another poem, the 'Rajaraja Vijaya' was presented on festival days. The representation of Siva as Tripurantaka is said to suggest a relationship to the conquering king, Rajaraja.

In all these ways the elevation to sacredness of the royal house was achieved, especially through the medium of the funerary temples. "It would therefore seem that the purpose of the Tanjavur temple as....a place where Cola rulers were given the status of 'divine beings', as well as the centre of the royal cult, was related to other efforts by Rajaraja I to use canonical religious forms to extend the scope of Cola royal authority with and beyond the Kaveri domain."[147]

SRI LANKA RELIGIOUS POLICY

Rajaraja conquered Sri Lanka in 991 A.D. and colonised it. It was not just a military raid but a regular conquest. He made it a province of the Cola empire, and renamed it Mummadi Cola Valanāḍu (after one of his own surnames). Anuradhapura, the capital of Ilam, an ancient fourishing city, was sacked, and a new capital was established at Polonnaruva. This city was renamed Jananathapuram. Several Siva temples were built under Rajaraja I, Rajendra I and Virarajendra. Here too, Rajaraja introduced the same uniformity in temple construction and modelled its administration after the administrative set-up of the mainland temples.

Between 991-1070 A.D., Ilam was under Cola rule. The Colas replicated in the island the organisation of townships, the building of Siva temples and the establishment of *brahmadēyas* on the same lines as on the mainland. The record in the 3rd year of Adhirajendra[148] states that a lamp was to be maintained from the interest on the deposit of money with the temple, and that the gift to be placed under the protection of *Māhēśvaras* and other members of the local committee (*patipādamulapaṭṭuḍai pañchāchāriya dēvakarmiikkaḷ*), including a Brahmana and some Siva Brahmanas. The insc. also refers to pipers (*uvachchar*), *paṉmāhēśvara-kankāni* of the temple and some dancing girls. It states that these members of the temple establishment, and after them their successors, priests, *parichārkar* (attendant service holders), *panmāhēśvara kankāṇi seyvār* (superintendent among priests), *nāṭṭavar* (of *nāḍu*) and dancing girls etc. were to ensure the service.

Vedic Brahmanas and Brahmana priests, especially of *nārpattennāyiram* group (widely spread in the Tamil country), pipers, dancing girls and attendants had all migrated to the conquered territory. The organisation of the temple establishment was similar to that on the mainland. Here too, tax-free land grants were made to the temples.[149]

The physical distance of these islands from the mainland and from the capital of Tanjavur in particular made it possible to free themselves from the political overlordship of the Colas at the slightest opportunity. Rajaraja and his successors were aware of such a possibility. They maintained military cantonments on the island and in strategic places all over the conquered territories. A military presence is essential to establish political authority. An administrative reorganisation is important to consolidate the political power of the conqueror. But a religious control over the colony would make it come under the ritual control of the mainland ideology. Even when the political control over the island became nebulous, the introduction of the new royal cult of Saivism through the establishment of agamic temples brought about an indirect hold over the colony. This, then, would be one of the prime reasons for the royal houses of the medieval period to establish the royal cult over the conquered territories, if we wonder why they should spend such large amounts to construct monumental temples in these places. Religion for them was not just a spiritual need, but used judiciously, helped to establish Cola hegemony over the conquered territories.

SECTION VII

THE ROYAL TEMPLE AND THE COLA ARMY

The Cola army was involved in several ways in administering the empire and the royal institutions. The active participation of the army in the civic life of the people was one way by which the kings ensured the support of the military to their government. The military officers were rewarded for their loyalty by being given high administrative positions in the government, as well as through land grants (*mānyams*). With time, these military officers became powerful local chiefs, who, in the last days of the Cola empire, proclaimed their independence as rulers of petty kingdoms. It was to the credit of Rajaraja I that he realised the power of a large, standing army and gave it due importance.

Apart from giving his military officers importance in administrative matters, Rajaraja encouraged them to participate in his religious institutions. During his reign and that of his successors, the army was involved in several ways in temple affairs: in administering some temples; by managing endowments in others; in helping the auditors to detect irregularities in financial transactions in temples; acting as guardians protecting the temples and their properties; making grants to temples etc. In these and other ways, the Cola kings brought about a close interaction between this important arm of the government and society through the medium of the temple.

First and foremost, we must establish the fact that the Cola army was a standing one, stationed in garrisons or cantonments. A standing army was of vital importance to the Cola kings, who were waging incessant wars against their neighbouring states to expand their frontiers. It was only with the help of a large regular army that control could be maintained over the conquered territories, which were often brought under the rule of a Cola governor. The size of the Cola army must have been considerable. A Western Calukyan inscription[150] at Hottur (in the Dharwar dist. of Karnataka state) states that the Cola army which fought under Rajendra I against Satyasraya consisted of nine lakh soldiers. If this were so, then the total strength of the army must have been considerably greater, taking into account his engagements in other sectors, such as the Pandya country, Malaināḍu, Vengi and Sri Lanka.

STEIN'S VIEWS

This is contrary to the observation of Burton Stein that the Cola army consisted of mercenaries or peasants and labourers, who fought when the occasion (*Vēlai*) demanded. He states, "the conquests of Cola rulers from Sundara Cola (A.D. 956-73) to Kulottunga I (A.D. 1070-1120) are real enough, but these conquests neither presuppose nor require a vast, standing army. Military power was possessed by numerous chiefs, by itinerant merchant groups and others throughout the Cola macro-region. These were locally recruited and controlled forces. It is one of the major flaws in the reading of Cola evidence to see armed force as the monopoly of the Cola kingship, and it is important to recognize that upon the specious notion of a vast, central and standing army, much of the justification for the Cola bureaucracy rests....It can be shown that there existed neither a centrally controlled military organization nor centrally coordinated redistribution of what were regarded as state resources. Military needs and the support of religious institutions and *Brāhmanas* were met from resources allocated by those under whose control such resources were: locality chieftains, not the Cola rulers, except as the latter were themselves locality leaders in the central parts of Kaveri basin."[151]

However, an analysis of inscriptional evidence proves that Stein's ideas are not justified. The evidence of the existence of '*kaḍagams*' or garrisons shows that army cantonments were established in different parts of the empire. These *kaḍagams* were also called *paḍaivīdus.* There are references to the *villigaḷ* (bowmen) of Enanallur-kadagam,[152] as also to troops quartered in Tiruvidaimarudil.[153] Mention is made of the Captain of the troops in this town: *Ivvūrp-paḍait-talaivār.*[154] Several small villages and hamlets bear names ending in *paḍaiyūr* or *paḍaivīḍu* (meaning the place where the army is stationed). A section of the army is called *pāṇḍippaḍai,* and is mentioned in an inscription of Parantaka I in the Nagesvara temple. A whole group of army men (*sēnaiyār*) was entrusted with the protection of the temple endowments at Tiruvidaimarudur.[155]

The mode of remuneration of the army is not specified; however, it is likely that a sizeable quantity of the booty from war would have been distributed among the army units. The booty captured in war was disposed of by the king at his will. However, this mode of payment would have been erratic and made the army depend solely on war spoils. It is more likely that a regular mode of payment for the army would have ensured a disciplined, well-organized military.

We are not concerned here so much with the mode of payment as we are about the manner in which the army was involved in temple affairs, especially after Rajaraja I's reign. In fact, the army regiments had a corporate life of their own and were free to make endowments or build temples. Through the inscriptions we learn more about the role that the army units played in civil life than about their military exploits.

The names of several regiments, units and divisions of the army give some idea of how and when they were formed. Though the methods of recruitment are not clear, nor is it clear that they were a highly trained professional outfit, having little or nothing in common with the civilian population; yet it can be stated that they were no mere rabble with little military training. The names of some 30 regiments mentioned in Rajaraja I's inscriptions have been collected by Venkayya.[156] Many of them have royal titles in the first portion of their names. Venkayya opines that they probably distinguished themselves in some engagement or other. Mention is made of the different sections of the army, like the elephant corps (*ānaiyāṭkaḷ*), the cavalry (*kudiraccēvagai*), *villigaḷ* (bowmen) etc.

The army units were divided on territorial lines, like *Pāṇḍi-paḍai,*[157] *Ten-Ilangai-Valañjiyar*[158] etc. That some of the army regiments had long and distinguished traditions and achievements to their credit is seen from the Tiruvalisvaram inscription[159] near Ambasamudaram in Tirunelveli District. (This undated inscription is assigned to the period of Rajaraja I and Rajendra I.) This regiment is called the *Mūnṛukai-Mahāsēnai* (the Great Army of the Three Arms or Sections). In the epigraph, it speaks with pride about its various conquests in several engagements—all under Rajaraja I and his successor, in which it distinguished itself. This army is also called the residents of Pandi-nadu. These armymen took under their eternal protection the temple of Tiruvalisvaram and all its belongings, its priests and servants. According to another record[160] from Seramadevi in 1096 A.D., this unit undertook to protect another temple and its properties, and calls itself "the several armed thousands of the great army of the three divisions (*Kai*)".

The mention of the 3 divisions (*mūnṛukai*) of the army is found in another record[161] from Polonnaruva of Vijayabahu I. Herein mention is made of the *Vēllaikāras,* who consisted of the 3 divisions of the *Mahātantra,* the *Valañjiyar* and the *Nagarattār* who were invited by the Sinhala king to protect the Buddhist temple for the tooth relic. The temple was renamed as *Mūnṛu-kai-tiru-Vēlaikkāran-Daḷadāy-perum-paḷḷi.* They bound themselves to protect the temple, its lands, its serfs and properties etc. The Mahavamsa[162] states that these *Vēlaikkāras* were brought to the Sri Lankan mainland by the conquering Cola kings, and were left behind to protect the Cola properties, including the temples built by the Colas; that they were a powerful community wooed by the Sinhala kings and that they were quite capable of creating problems like revolting against their masters.

Thus the interpretation of the term *mūnṛukai* is varied and interesting. If this same unit is also mentioned in the Tiruvalisvaram record mentioned above (as is quite possible, since they call themselves the residents of Pandināḍu), then the transformation and conversion of bodyguards or soldiers associated with the merchant guilds into a powerful regiment of the army, with a rich martial tradition was complete. In the Tanjavur inscription of Rajaraja I and Rajendra I, *Sirudanam* is the title of military officers. Sirudanam was also the honorary title of officers and private individuals. Among the regiments mentioned are *Sirudanattu-vaḍuga-kkāvalar* and *Sirdanattu-Valaṅgai-Velaikkāra-ppaḍaigaḷ.*

The *Kaikkōlas* are another section of the army. The *Kaikkōla-pperumbaḍai,*[163] the great troops of the *Kaikkōlas,* included all the regiments known as *Kaikkōlar.* Interpreted also as 'weavers',[164] Sastri feels that the term has a more literal meaning in the Cola epigraphs.[165] He states that it indicates 'a class of men distinguished by the strength of their arms', or 'the strong men of the wings (of the army)', that is, soldiers of the infantry division in the army. Some regiments of bowmen and swordsmen were called *Valpeṛṛa kaikkōlars.*

There are also references to another specialised regiment called *nāttuppaḍai paliyili ainnūṛṛuvār,* who are involved in maintaining a charitable endowment.[166] Who these faultless 500 were and what their relation to the rest of the *nāttuppaḍai* was, is not clear. Sastri points out that the two divisions of the army mentioned appear to have constituted two out of the four kinds of troops prescribed in the books of Indian polity—hereditary (*maula*), mercenary (*bhrtaka*), militia (*śrēni*), and tribal (*aṭāvi*).

ARMY'S ROLE IN TEMPLES

We already know of the involvement of local bodies in the management and administration of temples. We have also seen how the kings and their retinue, as well as royal officials and military officers made benefactions to temples and even assisted in their administration. However, in all these instances the officials (both military and civilian—the dividing line between them being very thin) acted in their individual capacity. In the case of temples built by royalty, especially of the size and reach of the Rajarajesvaram at Tanjavur, the endowments were made by the king and members of his royal household; by his important officers; by senior military officers or military regiments; by spiritual preceptors; by some influential merchants and a few other well-connected individuals. There are hardly any cases of endowments being made by ordinary people. All those associated with the temple were people of some standing in society. The 'elitist' nature of the royal temple was thus ensured.

By involving the army in temple matters, the king ensured its commitment to the upkeep and protection of its undertakings. In the Tanjavur temple, the military was involved in several ways. Icons were set up by some important military officers, and endowments made to them in the form of gold or silver ornaments and vessels. Cash grants by army officers were invested with the *sabhās* by the temple authorities. Endowments for maintaining lamps in the temple were made by several people, including army officers. Finally, punishment was meted out to the erring officers by the king, in the form of compulsory endowments for lamps.

Although, military officers were not actively involved in the administration of the Tanjavur temple, there were several temples where the army's role in managing them was encouraged by the rulers. Even in the case of the Tanjavur temple, certain shrines were maintained and managed by the armymen. One of the officers Krishnan Raman whose title was Mummadi Brahmarayar Niyomam was the Senapati. He was an important Commander-in-Chief of Rajaraja's. (The Larger Leyden Copper Plate tells us about him.[167]) He became the *Tirumandira Ōlaināyagam* which was the highest post in the bureaucratic set-up of Rajaraja and Rajendra. Krishnan Raman outlived Rajaraja I and served his son and successor Rajendra I, under whom he took the title of Rajendrasola Brahmamarayan, in keeping with the tradition in vogue then of adopting the current ruler's name. He was a *perundanam* of Rajaraja I. It is significant that a Brahmana military officer rose to the rank of

C-in-C and it is equally important to note that the top civilian posts were entrusted to high-ranking officers of the army.

Krishnan Raman is also among the donors of the Tanjavur temple. He constructed the inner wall of the enclosure round the Rajarajesvaram temple, as is evidenced by three inscriptions[168] on its southern and western wings. This wall called the *'Krishnan Raman Tiru-churru-māligai'* with the Rajarajatiru-Vasal, and immediately outer wall of enclosure with the Keralantaka-tiru-vasal, i.e., the walls of fortification with the bastions and the moat around, are mentioned in the Tivuviśaippa of Karur Devar, the *guru* of Rajaraja I. Incidentally, this seems to be the first example of such defence works in any South Indian temple. A metal image of Ardhanarisvarar was set up by him in the temple before the 29th year of Rajaraja I, and he endowed it with jewels.[169]

Similarly, another important officer, Irayiravan Pallavayar alias Mummadisola Posan, set up an image in copper of Chandesvara Devar, before the 29th year of the king and presented it with certain ornaments.[170] Pallavayar was a *perundanam* of Rajaraja I.

Military officers aided in auditing temple accounts. For example in the 3rd year of Adhirajendradeva and the 8th and 21st year of Kulottunga, there were cases of embezzlement discovered in the Arunajatesvara Temple in Tiruppandal in Kumbakonam dist. These cases of misdemeanour by the temple treasurers were inspected by Rajaraja MVN Senapati Pallavarayar and Senapati Nandiyarajar respectively.[171]

MANAGEMENT OF SHRINES

The army units were entrusted with the management of some shrines in the Tanjavur Temple. The units made cash grants to the temple which were lent out on interest to various *sabhās* in Colamandalam. Out of this income, several services were conducted. An analysis of some of the army units which were attached to the Rajarajesvaram and cash grants made by them to *sabhās* is given in Table 9. The table shows the financial resources commanded by various army regiments and how they were actively involved in the management of various shrines within the Tanjavur Temple. The enclosed table has been prepared from the following inscs.: SII, II, 9, 12-19, 35, 54.

In two sets of inscs. (SII, II, 63 & 64; 94 & 95) several military officers have made grants for maintaining lamps in the temple. As has already been stated, this record gives the names of the 14 military officers who made grants under duress. They atoned for their defeat in the Kōḻi debacle by maintaining lamps in the temple. These officers gave in all 800 ewes towards maintaining several lamps. Among them, Perundaram Uttarangudaiyan Kon Vidividangan seems to have given the maximum (114 *kāśus* for 342 ewes).

Using the medium of the royal temple to serve punishments on erring officials (civilian and military) was yet another way in which the army was bound to the royal institution and made to get involved in temple matters. The religious medium of the temple was used to serve punishments. By serving their sentence in the temple, these officers were assured of getting back into the king's favour.

Apart from the military officers who were punished, there were others who made grants for lamps purely for merit, as well as to curry the favour of the king. A list of these officers is given in the table in Sec. III.

Herein, we have evidence of the manner in which the kings kept their military officers in check and in constant fear against any misdemeanour on their part. Fear of royal disapproval kept powerful military chieftains under control and discouraged personal ambitions from surfacing (at least when the Cola kings were powerful). Loyalty to the king and empire and to the royal institutions was the paramount guiding principle.

The participation of the military in certain aspects of civil administration is thus well attested. It ensured that the army was never idle. At the same time, Rajaraja I and his successors kept military ambitions under control in the ways delineated above. The royal temple was, thus, a useful institution to engage the military in various economic and welfare activities of the government. We have seen how resources from the military sector were redistributed to the agricultural sector; and how the wealth acquired through wars came to be invested in the countryside via the medium of the royal temple.

TABLE 9

No.	Army Unit	For the Image of	To Sabhā	Amount in Kāśu
1.	Valangai-Parambadaigalilar (Right-Hand Troops)	Biksadevar (set up by Queen Lokamahadevi)	Nedumanal (Madanamanjari CVM in Nenmalināḍu)	252
2.	Regiment Niyayam Perundanattu Valangai-Velaikkara Padaigal	Main Deity		
	Contingents:	Palliyil (Nenmalināḍu)		31
	a. Pandita-Sola-terinda villaligal			
	b. Rajavinoda-terinda-valangai-velaikkarar	Perumbalamarudur (Purangaranbaināḍu)		310
	c. Pandita-Sola-terinda-villaliyar	- do -		267
	d. Chandraparakrama-terinda-valangai-velaikkarar	- do -		223
	e. Nittavinoda-terinda-valangai-velaikkarar	Palliyil (Nenmalināḍu)		13
3.	Niyayam-Sirudanattu Valangai-Velaikkara-Padaigalilar	Dakshina Meru Vitakar	a. Kalappal (Purangarambai nāḍu)	125
	- do -	- do -	b. Kori (Purangarambai nāḍu)	300
	- do -	- do -	c. Vanganagar (same nāḍu)	500
	- do -	- do -	d. Arinjigai CVM	800
			e. Kundavai CVM	500
			f. Panaiyur (Purangarambai nāḍu)	500
4.	Niyayam-Uttama-Sola-terinda-andalagattalar	Chandesvara (set up by a Perundaram)	Palliyil (Nenmalināḍu)	60
5.	Military Officers		Sri-Viranarayana CVM (taniyur)	743
6.	Military Officers		Perumakkalur (Kirar-Kurram)	120

SECTION VIII

CONCLUSIONS

The study of the royal temple of Rajarajesvaram helps to highlight the arguments put forth in this thesis, that the royal temple was an institution with considerable power and influence. The royal temple in the Middle Cola period was not just a temple used by the king and his royal household, but was an arm of the government and as such, wielded influence and control over the entire empire including the conquered territories. The manner in which the royal temple was effectively used to establish and consolidate Cola hegemony is brought out in the various sections; each of which discusses and analyses a particular aspect of the Rajarajesvaram as an instrument of the government. The uniqueness of the temple as a royal institution is shown in the range of its activities.

From a study of its administrative arrangements, it is clear that this was no ordinary temple, but a monumental undertaking of the greatest kind of South India. The size of the administration of the Rajarajesvaram made it the largest temple of its time. More than 800 persons were on its rolls; many more were tied to it indirectly. The livelihood of such a large body of persons centred around this unique institution. The administration of the other temples of the time was much smaller and less elaborate. It was the Middle Colas under Rajaraja and his son Rajendra, who had the power and the resources to make the administration of their royal temples the biggest and most efficient in South India. The rationality in the appointments to the administrative body illustrates the deep study made into the powers and responsibilities of various posts and the clear-cut delineation of powers ensured that no ambiguity was created in the discharge of duties.

All the appointments were made by the government. The chief manager in charge of the administration of the temple, the Śrikāryam, was a high-ranking Cola official and the headman of a village. Only persons with landed property and wealth were appointed to key posts like those of the chief supervisor, the accountants, the treasurers etc. To these persons the salary or income from the temple was not so important; their appointment to the administration of the royal temple was compensation enough. Most non-royal and *bhakti* temples drew their staff from the nearby localities and were managed and administered for the most part by the local bodies. Appointments from far-off places were rare. However, in the case of the royal temple of Tanjavur the areas surrounding Tanjavur were not given undue importance in its management. The local bodies had no say whatsoever in the affairs of the temple.

The economy of medieval temples embraced a wide spectrum of activities. The temples were wealthy institutions with considerable property in land, cash, gold, cattle, etc. Proper finance management was, therefore, important to ensure a steady revenue to defray the salaries of its staff and to pay for the various services, festivals, renovations and additions to the structure, etc. The income of temples was mainly revenue from land grants and from cash grants, which was, in turn, lent out on interest (to assemblies, groups or individuals).

Rajaraja made extensive land grants to the Rajarajesvaram, yielding a large revenue in kind and in cash. The revenue from land grants to this temple exceeded that of several large-sized temples. This was so because Rajaraja granted entire villages (almost 40 in Colamandalam), instead of portions of villages, which usually constituted the land grants to other temples. These 40 villages were converted into *dēvadāna* by Rajaraja, using his imperial authority to hand-pick only those villages which yielded a uniform rate of assessment (i.e. 100 *kalams* per *vēli*). There is no mention here of the land being acquired from others on the payment of a lumpsum tax known as *pūrvācāram* or *iṛai-dravyam.* He granted the lands in his capacity as the emperor of the Cola empire.

The cash grants to the temple were made by the king, his family, his religious gurus, army officers, civil officials and high-ranking temple staff. There are no commoners among the donors. The cash amounts were lent out by the finance section of the temple only to *sabhās* and not to groups or individuals. This was because the amounts lent out were large and could be borrowed mainly by village assemblies. The income from the interest was outlaid for specific items to be procured for the temple.

The large number of cattle granted for maintaining lamps in the temple was also unheard of in its time. Rajaraja and his retinue lavished their wealth in maintaining special lamps like *nundaviḷakku* (perpetual lamps) and *sandhi viḷakku* (twilight lamps). This grant established a service relationship between the temple and the shepherds—whose services were requisitioned by the temple to supply it with ghee, milk, curd, etc. The shepherds who benefited by these grants were placed not only in and around Tanjavur, but were distributed all over the empire—in Rajaraja VN and even in Vaḍa Kōnāḍu. An interesting feature of these grants was the involvement of a large number of top-ranking military officers, who seem to have made lamp grants under some kind of duress. The royal temple was thus used to mete out punishment to erring military officers. This grant is also significant in showing the redistribution of resources from the military sector to the agrarian (or pastoral) sector.

From a significant record we learn that Rajaraja granted sixteen villages to the Rajarajesvaram. These villages were situated outside the core region of Colamandalam and their importance lies, not so much in the area or revenue granted, but in their location. All these villages lie in the territories conquered by Rajaraja. Again entire villages were granted. Rajaraja exercised his authority in making these grants of fairly large-sized villages in places as far away from Tanjavur as Anantapur (in present day Andhra Pradesh), and assigning several taxes to the royal temple. Yet another aspect of these grants is the statement that 'the previous owners were replaced' in all the villages (except those in Ilam). Some of the villages granted to the Tanjavur temple seem to have been *dēvadānas* and *brahmadēyas.* As a rule, the owners were compensated, the villages were converted to *vēllān-vagai* and only then were they granted as *dēvadāna.* No such procedure is mentioned in these grants. All these point to the arbitrary authority of the imperial Colas in interfering with land relationships in the areas conquered by them. Thus, the royal government exercised political control over the conquered territories through the medium of the royal temple.

The fairly long insc. appointing various staff to the Rajarajesvaram provides an insight into the manner in which the royal government could draw upon the best talents available in the kingdom and transfer them *en masse* to the royal temple. The *brahmadēyas* were ordered to provide qualified personnel like accountants, treasurers, *brahmacarins,* watchmen etc. and to pay the salaries to some of them (out of the tax dues of the villages). The grant shows the arbitrary manner in which the government under the medieval Colas could make appointments and transfer people from different parts of the kingdom to the Tanjavur temple. The government could interfere in the management and staff appointments of non-royal and *bhakti* temples, without offering any compensation. The responsibility of remunerating some of the staff like watchmen was transferred to the local bodies. The royal temple was also used as a symbol of overriding power over the *brahmadēyas* of Colamandalam. These Brahmana villages wielded much influence from early times. But, their interest was subordinated to that of the royal temple as a result of this grant. Each one of the appointments was meticulously made, the salary and perquisites stated in detail and the nature of appointment, whether hereditary or not, specified. These are pointers to the high level of organisation of the royal government under Rajaraja.

The royal patronage to a chosen form of Saivism was implemented through the institution of the royal temple. All major royal undertakings were to Siva. The properties of some non-Saiva temples, especially Jaina *paḷḷis,* were made over to the royal temple. The Colas propagated the cult of the *liṅga* and established *liṅgas* in the sanctums of all Siva temples. The patronage given to *maṭhas* and *maṭha* heads, and the influence of the preceptors of the Golaki *maṭha* helped in the royal endeavour. Henceforth, worship was conducted strictly according to the *āgamas.* New iconographic innovations helped to establish the supremacy of Siva over Visnu and the other gods. The institutionalisation of the *Tēvaram* hymns by the Middle Colas and the festivals in honour of the saints led to their canonisation. The royal temple was thus used to spread the religious beliefs and cults practised by the Colas within Colamandalam and even in conquered territories like Ilam.

The involvement of the Cola bureaucracy and military in the royal temple was achieved in several ways. Rajaraja managed to get his army actively involved in the royal undertaking. This was achieved in several ways, like making the regiments responsible for the services in the temple. The royal officers built some portions of the temple and added to the main structure, set up images, donated cash and gold to the temple as well as undertook to maintain lamps. The king also used the royal temple to mete out punishment to erring military officers.

The territorial reach of the Rajarajesvaram exceeded that of any temple known till its time. The land grants covered a vast area in Colamandalam and outside the core region; the influence of the temple encompassed the whole of peninsular South India, and even spilt over to Ilam. Thus, the influence of the royal temple was far-reaching. The recruitment of its staff was also from every part of Colamandalam.

More than any other department of the Cola government, it was the royal temple of Rajarajesvaram, encompassing the Cola empire in various ways, which demonstrated the imperial authority and through which social, economic, political and religious control was sought to be exercised over the entire empire.

APPENDIX

THE ROYAL TEMPLE AND THE BRAHMADĒYAS

What is significant in most of these orders, is that they are addressed to *brahmadēyas*. While in the case of the accountants, treasurers and *Brāhmana* servants, the *brahmadēyas* were ordered to supply to the temple the above-mentioned temple servants; in the case of the watchmen, the *brahmadēyas* had not only to supply them to the temple, but also pay them their remuneration in the form of paddy. This paddy and daily allowances, every year, were to be paid by the inhabitants of the respective *brahmadēyas* out of their tax dues.

Burton Stein[172] has mapped the distribution pattern of some 300 *brahmadēya* villages of the Cola period, which could be located more or less accurately. The existence of more *Brāhmana* villages cannot be ruled out, as records pertaining to them have been lost, or some *brahmadēyas* cannot simply be located. In Stein's study, "the most significant concentration occurs in the riverine tracts of the Kaveri and its tributaries, the Ponnaiyar, the Western Tamraparani and the Palar." Most *brahmadēyas* lie below the 250 ft contour; while the others follow the major river basins through the graded descent from higher elevations to the sea-level plains below. Therefore, the *Brāhmana* villages were located mainly in those areas where natural irrigation facilities were easily available. Thus, it is important to note that "the *Brāhmana* village is a reliable and accurate 'marker' of the most mature agrarian localities in the macro-region. The high consumption requirements of these villages were supportable only under the most advanced conditions of agriculture. Moreover, these same localities, it must be presumed, bore the highest burden of tribute payments."[173]

This is one reason why the order to supply and maintain temple personnel was addressed only to *brahmadēyas*. No doubt, the ultimate burden was on the government, which decided to forgo a part of the tax dues from the *brahmadēyas*. This was now converted as payments to the watchmen by the respective villages. The tax dues of *brahmadēya* villages would have been substantial enough for the government to forgo a portion of it. Therefore, these orders were addressed only to *brahmadēyas*. Besides, the required qualified *Brāhmana* functionaries for the temple could be recruited mostly from the numerous *brahmadēyas*.

The question of whether it was only the *brahmadēyas* which were rich enough to provide temple functionaries, is interesting. *Vēllān-vagai* villages were not asked to supply and maintain any permanent staff for the royal temple. As already stated, only *vēllān-vagai* villages were converted into *dēvadāna* lands. In these villages, the *mēlvāram* was being paid to the government and this was now transferred to the temple concerned.

"The terms *vēllān-vagai* and *brahmadēya* refer to categories of major recipients of agricultural income. *Vēllān-vagai*, a sharing of agricultural income among cultivating peoples, peasant families comprising the various *ūrār* of the *nāḍu*; *brahmadēya*, a sharing of income among *Brāhmana* families under the authority of the *sabhā*."[174] As already noted, *brahmadēyas* were created in all high-yielding agricultural tracts. This meant that the income from these special villages was much higher than that of the *vēllān-vagai* villages. This is not to state categorically that all fertile tracts were converted into *brahmadēyas*; though a fair portion of the high-yielding areas was under *brahmadēya* control. It is significant that all the orders for the supply and remuneration of temple staff were addressed to *brahmadēyas*. This implied that the tax dues of the *brahmadēyas* were fairly high, again pointing to high-yielding areas. Also, the order that the *brahmadēyas* should supply accountants and treasurers is significant, for it shows that the requisite qualified staff were to be found mainly in the *brahmadēyas*. All these facts point to a higher revenue generation and a more mature division of labour in the *brahmadēyas*. Most *brahmadēyas* seem to be, thus, better organised and better-off financially than the average *vēllān-vagai* village. Karashima.[175] in his study of two adjoining villages in Trichy district, Isanamangalam[176] a *brahmadēya* and Allur[177] (a non-*brahmadēya* village), has analysed the land ownership tenure and social stratification of the community.

In a table from the same study,[178] among the donors or sellers of land (to the donors or to the temples), 82% are *Brāhmanas* among individual sellers. This, in itself, speaks of the *brahmadēyas* being wealthy in land. This situation was reversed to a certain extent, in the later Cola period, when individual *kāni* holders became wealthy landholders and the pre-eminent position of the *Brāhmana* landholders of the *brahmadēyas* diminished to a certain extent.

By addressing his order to the *brahmadēyas* in Colamandalam, Rajaraja acknowledged their financial capability to support the staff appointed to the temple, as well as the availability of qualified and learned *Brāhmanas* living in them. These *Brāhmana* villages were quite wealthy in land and men. At the same time, they enjoyed many privileges granted to them by the kings themselves. Some of the *sabhās* became quite influential in course of time. (This was also the transitionary period, when power was shifting from the *sabhās* to temples.) However, by making it obligatory for the *brahmadēyas* to support the royal undertaking, Rajaraja exercised his imperial power in curbing the independence of the *brahmadēyas.*

REFERENCES

1. Sastri, The Cholas, Ch. IX, p. 168.
2. S.R. Balasubramanyam, Middle Chola Temples.
3. SII, II, pt. 5 Introduction by Venkayya.
4. Sastri, Malaviya Commemoration Volume, p. 143.
5. Mooka Reddy, The Tirumalavadi Temple, p. 35.
6. Ibid.
7. B. Venkatraman, Rajarajesvaram, p. 231ff.
8. SII, II, 61.
9. I.P.S., No. 285.
10. I.P.S., No. 336.
11. SII, XIV, 95.
12. SII, VIII, 277.
13. SII, XIV, 95.
14. SII, II, 26.
15. SII, II, 38.
16. SII, II, 36.
17. Pudukottai Glossary, p. 359.
18. SII, II, 69.
19. SII, XIV, 95.
20. K.V. Raman, Sri Varadarajasvami Temple, p. 120.
21. SII, XXIV, 244.
22. SII, II, 68.
23. SII, II, 88.
24. S.R. Balasubramanyam, Early Chola Art, p. 29.
25. K.V. Subramanya Aiyer, Historical Sketches of Ancient Dekhan, Vol. I, p. 333.
26. K.V. Soundararajan, The Art of South India, p. 14.
27. SII, XIX, 137; SII, XIII, 642, 638, 633.
28. SII, II, 68.
29. K.V. Ramesh, "Epigraphy...".

30. SII, II, 66.
31. SII, II, 57.
32. SII, II, 11.
33. SII, II, 20.
34. Sastri, Malaviya Commemoration Vol., p. 143.
35. SII, II, 95.
36. S.R. Balasubramanyam, op. cit., p. 29.
37. SII, II, 68.
38. Rajamanickam, Saivism, p. 144.
39. SII, II, 69.
40. SII, II, 65.
41. SII, II, 66.
42. Ibid.
43. 128 of 1912.
44. SII, II, 66.
45. S.R. Balasubramanyam, op. cit., p. 75.
46. SII, II, 66.
47. SII, II, 67.
48. SII, II, 62.
49. Sastri, op. cit.
50. SII, II, 4, 5. "Udaiyar sri Rajarajadevar Tanjavur edupitta tiru-karrali Sri Rajarajesvaram udaiyar Paramasvamikku vendu nivandangalikkut devadanamagach cholamandalattum puramandalangalilum udaiyar sri Rajarajadevar kudutta..."
51. S.R. Balasubramanyam, op. cit., p. 70.
52. SII, II, 68.
53. SII, II, 4.
54. Ibid.
55. Noburu Karashima, South Indian History & Society, Ch. III, pt. 2 (for a study on the revenue system and land grants).
56. SII, II, 5.
57. SII, III, 205.
58. SII, II, 5.
59. Karashima, op. cit.
60. SII, II, Introduction, p. 17, 255 of 1921.
61. SII, II, 9.
62. SII, II, 10, 11.
63. SII, II, 63, 64, 94, 95.
64. Arjun Appadurai, Conflicts..., Ch. II, p. 71.
65. S.R. Balasubramanyam, op. cit., p. 82 (for details).
66. SII, II, 95, No. 2.
67. SII, II, 6, No. 18.
68. SII, II, 6, No. 24.
69. 551 of 1919.
70. "Nal onrukku tirumadapalliyil alakkum ariyanavallan naliyal nei ulakkum, tayir amudu-naliyum" (551 of 1919).

71. Konadu is an ancient Tamil country. Kodumbalur in Pudukottai Dist. was its chief town. Nayanar King, Idaigari-Nayanar, was the ruler of this region. It was probably named so because it was a settlement of the Konars or shepherds. The names of several shepherds ended in Kon. For example Perumal-Kon, Damodara-Kon etc. (K.V. Raman, op. cit., p. 134).
72. T.R. Vasantha Bai, History of Thanjavur Through the Ages, p. 134.
73. SII, II, 64, 95.
74. George W. Spencer, "Temple Money-Lending...".
75. K.V. Raman, op. cit., p. 134.
76. Spencer, "Royal Initiative Under Rajaraja I".
77. SII, II, 95.
78. Kathleen Gough, "Modes of Production in Southern India".
79. SII, II, 92.
80. SII, II, 45.
81. SII, II, 92, Introduction by Venkayya.
82. 331 of 1927.
83. 79 of 1921.
84. Tiruvalangadu Plates.
85. M.A.R., 1917, p. 42.
86. 394 of 1911.
87. 97 of 1921; P. Shanmugam, The Revenue System of the Colas, p. 96.
88. SII, II, 92.
89. 395 of 1922.
90. SII, II, 1, paras 34, 51.
91. SII, III, pt. III, 205.
92. 361 of 1910.
93. SII, II, 92, para 12.
94. 612 of 1912.
95. SII, II, 91, 93.
96. Karashima, op. cit., p. 11; SII, VIII, 687-689, 692-94, 95, 96, 98, 99.
97. SII, II, 69.
98. SII, II, 57, 70.
99. SII, II, 66.
100. Vanamamalai, "State & Religion...", *Social Scientist.*
101. B. Venkataraman, op. cit., Table based on App. 18, 19.
102. R. Champakalakshmi, "Ideology and the State in South India".
103. Hocart, Kings and Councillors, p. 86.
104. K.V. Raman, Some Aspects of Pandyan History.
105. R. Nagaswamy, "New Light on Mamallapuram".
106. K.V. Raman, "Religious Trends During Rajaraja's Reign".
107. Anbil Plates.
108. Lawrence P. Briggs, The Ancient Khmer Empire, p. 25.
109. Ibid.
110. SII, II, 1.
111. Ibid.
112. R. Nagaswamy, "Saivism Under Rajaraja—A Study".

113. SII, II, 4.
114. SII, XIII, 13; 222 of 1911.
115. 212, 214, 217 of 1911.
116. Sastri, The Colas, p. 644.
117. R. Champakalakshmi, op. cit.
118. T.A. Gopinatha Rao, Elements of Hindu Iconography, Vol. II.
119. K.V. Soundararajan, Glimpses of Indian Culture, Architecture, Art & Religion, Introduction, p. XIX.
120. J.N. Banerjea, Development of Hindu Iconography, p. 463.
121. Burton Stein, Peasant State..., p. 337.
122. Rajamanickam, Saivism.
123. Sivaprakasam, Saiva Mathas.
124. 152 & 210 of 1929.
125. Rajamanickam, op. cit., Ch. IX.
126. 40 of 1906.
127. 189 of 1928-29.
128. 38 of 1944-45.
129. SII, II, 9.
130. SII, II, 27.
131. SII, II, 61.
132. S.R. Balasubramanyam, op. cit., p. 27.
133. SII, III, pt. 1, p. 93.
134. S.R. Balasubramanyam, op. cit., p. 77ff.
135. Ibid.
136. 97 of 1932.
137. 143-4, 149, 160-1 of 1940-1.
138. SII, II, 65.
139. D.G.E. Hall, A History of S-E Asia, p. 93.
140. B.R. Chaterjee, Indian Cultural Influence in Cambodia, p. 72.
141. S.R. Balasubramanyam, Early Chola Art, p. 20.
142. SII, III, 15-17.
143. SII, III, 18.
144. 289, 290 of 1978-79.
145. Ibid.
146. SII, II, 67.
147. Stein, op. cit., p. 339.
148. Ibid.
149. R. Tirumalai, "Glimpses of Cola Township in Sri Lanka".
150. S.R. Balasubramanyam, op. cit., p. 5.
151. Stein, Peasant State..., Ch. VII, pp. 257-58.
152. 394 of 1921.
153. 242 of 1907.
154. T.A.S., IV, pp. 134-5.
155. 239 of 1907; SII, XIII, 7.
156. SII, II, 5, Introduction by Venkayya.
157. 255 of 1911.

158. A.R. on Epigraphy for 1923, p. 106.
159. 120 of 1905.
160. 189 of 1895.
161. E.I., XVIII, 38.
162. Mahavamsa, Ch. LX.
163. 253 of 1907.
164. SII, II, p. 390, No. 6.
165. Sastri, The Colas, Ch. XVIII, p. 454.
166. 253 of 1904.
167. E.I., V, 34.
168. SII, II, 31, 33, 45.
169. SII, II, 39.
170. SII, II, 55.
171. 46 of 1914.
172. Stein, Peasant State..., p. 150.
173. Ibid, p. 144.
174. Ibid.
175. N. Karashima, op. cit., Ch. I, p. 9ff.
176. SII, VIII, 600-630.
177. Ibid, 687-88, 89-92, 98-99.
178. Karashima, op. cit., p. 13.

Chapter III

NON-ROYAL TEMPLE OF THE CORE REGION—TIRUVARUR

The main objective of this chapter is to make a close comparative study of a major non-royal *bhakti* temple in the core region of Colamandalam. Colamandalam has innumerable temples whose praises have been sung by the Saiva *nāyanārs*. Of them, some continue to be simple and modest in their size; while some have grown into bigger complexes with a number of enclosures, shrines, *mandapas* and *gōpuras*, thanks to the support received from both royal patrons and the common people. A detailed study of the Rajarajesvaram at Tanjavur has been attempted in the earlier pages. In order to compare and contrast such a royal temple with a holy temple, it is important that we choose, from among the myriad temples of Tanjavur district, a temple of equal size and importance, which will make such a comparison meaningful.

It is with this in mind that the Tyagarajaswami Temple of Tiruvarur has been chosen as a case-study. This temple is part of an enormous complex, therefore, it can match the Rajarajesvaram in size. It is a holy temple, sung by several *bhakti* saints and mentioned in many literary and religious works. Its evolution can be traced back in time to the primitive religious beliefs like ophiolatry and tree-worship. Its gradual conversion and growth as a Saiva centre can be traced. Its importance as a place of pilgrimage was mainly due to its association with the *bhakti* saints. It received patronage both from the royalty and the common people. Tiruvarur was traditionally one of the five secondary capitals of the Colas. The royal house involved itself in the temple primarily out of *bhakti*. Finally, its reach or influence, economically and socially, can be gauged from the 60 odd inscs., mostly of the Cola period, found on its walls. Thus, the Tiruvarur Temple can be successfully used as a model for comparison.

ANTIQUITY OF THE TEMPLE

Tiruvarur is in the Nagapattinam taluk of Tanjavur District on the banks of the Ōḍambōkki, a branch of the Kaveri in the delta region. The temple complex occupies an area of about 20 acres with the Kamalalaya tank to its west. There are numerous shrines and *mandapas* in the three spacious enclosures (*prākāra*). The two main shrines of the temple complex are the Valmikinathar and the Tyagarajar. Of the two, the former is the more ancient, and derives its name from the anthill (*puṟṟu*), which takes the place of the *liṅga* in the main shrine. In fact, Appar refers to the main deity in his hymns as *puṟṟidērikoṇḍān* (one who resides in an anthill).[1] The *sthala-vrksa* is the *patiri* (trumpet-flower tree). The principles and practices of tree-worship and ophiolatry are ancient bases whereupon at a later date the *liṅga* worship seems to have been established.[2]

The Tyagaraja shrine is the second oldest in this temple, which has altogether four important shrines, all dedicated to Siva. The image of Tyagaraja is a metal one and consists of the Somaskanda group. (This deity is referred to as Vīdiviṭankar in the Cola inscs.) The name, Tyagaraja, figures only from the 15th-16th c. onwards. The original names were Vīdiviṭankar in Tamil and Arurādhipati in Sanskrit. A 7th year record of Rajaraja I states that the Tiruvarur Temple was rebuilt in stone by Sembiyam Madevi. This deity has been eulogised in the *bhakti* poems (*Tēvaram*) of the saints, Appar, Nanasambandar and Sundarar. Sundarar sang his famous *Tiru-Tondait-Togai* here, which was the original source for Sekkilar's *Tiru-Tondar-Puranam.*[3] Thus, this temple is sanctified by intimate associations with the foremost of *bhakti* saints.

Right from the days of Appar, certain festivals are mentioned in the Tyagaraja shrine at Tiruvarur. The *Tiruvādirai* and *Uttiram* festivals have been mentioned in Appar's works and continue to be celebrated still. The Cola record of the 12th c.[4] mentions large provisions for these festivals. The fact that the deity, Tyagaraja, is a metal image and was originally an *utsava-mūrti*, attests to the antiquity of these festivals.

As already mentioned, the fact that the anthill was later worshipped as a *liṅga*, speaks of the antiquity of this temple complex. The oldest shrine was that of Valmikinathar. The Tyagaraja shrine was built at a later date. Both these shrines share a common *mahāmandapa.* They are surrounded by the first enclosure (*prākāra*). This *prākāra* has a three-storeyed *gōpuram.* In the second enclosure lies the Achalesvara shrine. This shrine was a foundation of Sembiyam Madevi, and therefore, belongs to the middle Cola period. Within the second enclosure are the other shrines to Siva, the Atakesvara shrine, the Anandesvarar shrine and the Siddisvarar shrine—all constructed during a later period (one of them being an all-brick structure). A big hall known as the Rajanarayana Tirumandapa (named after Kulottunga I) lies between the first and the second *prākāras.* The Amman shrine is also a later construction. There is a *gōpuram* on this wall too. In the third *prākāra* are two *mandapas,* one being the *Dēvaśrayan-mandapam.* It is said that this hall has original associations with Sundarar's *Tiru-Tondai-Togai* and was rebuilt in stone in the later Cola period.[5] The *gōpuram* on the third wall is said to have been built during the time of Kulottunga III, therefore, in the 13th c. A.D.[6] Most of the expansion, including the construction of the Amman shrine, was executed during the days of Kulottunga I when the campus of the temple expanded considerably. A later Vijayanagara record dated 1440 A.D. mentions the construction of the western *gōpuram* over the second *prākāra.* During the days of the Maratta King, Sarfoji, certain repairs were made.

Thus, we see a progressive growth of the temple campus. This is in sharp contrast to the royal temples like the *Rajarajesvaram,* where, apart from an additional Amman shrine, the temple complex remains almost bereft of later additions and continues in the very same form in which it was first visualised and planned by its builder.

We have, however, to acknowledge the fact that no temple (no matter how important it is) can be built into a great structure purely on its own income or through the benefactions of the common man alone. The role played by the kings and their royal retinue in increasing the size of the campus cannot be discounted. The *bhakti* temples through their sanctity kept alive the ardour of successive dynasties and thus ensured a continuity in their evolution. Even a great holy temple like Tirupati had its campus expanded and various festivals initiated due to the patronage of the kings of the Vijayanagara empire. A similar picture has emerged in the case of Sri Varadarajasvami Temple, Kanci.

Thus in Tiruvarur, too, we see considerable activities by the kings and their royal retinue. They built additional structures; repaired old ones; endowed gold, cash and land, etc. The sacred temples have grown with the times, each generation adding or contributing something to it as acts of piety; whereas the royal temples were largely one-time or one-person creations without much community involvement. While the former was revered as a holy institution steeped in some unknown or mystique antiquity, the latter was the creation of a mortal and hence lacked that reverence or holiness. They had a differential impact on the minds of the people and hence invoked differential response. A very important point of difference is that, while in royal temples the temple management or administration was directly done by the king's government, the non-royal temples were managed by the local, village assemblies or local people (*stanattār*, etc.).

LAND GRANTS

The land grants account for a majority of the endowments. Even for maintaining lamps, grants in land were made. Land grants were usually made by paying the tax dues to the villages from where the land was bought, and transferring the land to the temple as *dēvadāna.* The significant aspect of the endowments is that most of the land grants were made by private individuals or by village assemblies. The temple had quite a few villages (or lands in them) granted to it within a radius of 12 miles of Tiruvarur. This should be noted, because it emphasises the localised nature of the *bhakti* temple. Only such areas that were within manageable distance from the temple-town were granted to the temple for the following reasons. Firstly, the patronage of the *bhakti* temple was essentially from the locality around it. Therefore, most of the grants were made by individuals and assemblies of nearby villages. Secondly, the *bhakti* temple, unlike its royal counterpart, would not have been able to command the administrative machinery to collect dues from, or supervise lands granted in far-away villages. That is the reason why most of the endowed lands were within manageable distance of the temple concerned. Many *bhakti* temples developed into pilgrimage centres. As such, they did attract offerings from pilgrims in the form of cash, and sometimes, even land grants were made by them. However, these lands were located close to the temple; even individuals (royal officers and the like) who did not belong to the Tiruvarur region, made grants of land or villages near the temple.

The earliest record[7] in the temple refers to a land grant of 3 *vēlis* of land at Menmangalam by an individual. This is an insc. belonging to the 20th year of Aditya I.

A grant made by a dancing girl (*nakkaṉ*) was recorded during the reign of Rajadhiraja I.[8] This lady, called Anukkiyar Paravai Nangaiyar, built a *mandapam* in this temple, called *Rajendrasolan-tirumandapam.* She also donated vast quantities of gold and copper for gilding the *vimāna* over the sanctum. She seems to have been a favourite of Rajendra I and shared the temple honours with him. She had granted several bits of lands in the villages of Tīyankuḍi and Mēnmangalam, which were bought over jointly by the king and herself for expenses in the temple. This is an instance of a grant made by the king and his retinue.

A significant royal grant[9] was made during the reign of Kulottunga II. It is a royal order for making provisions to the images of Sambandar and Sundarar in the Valmikinatha shrine, as well as additional grants for conducting festivals. According to this order, two *brahmadēya* villages, Tiruvadiraimangalam and Amur, were joined and renamed as Anapayanallūr (Anapaya being the name of Kulottunga II). It also states that huge chunks from two villages, Gangaikondasolanallur and Arangamangalam, were joined together to form another *dēvadāna* village, Dānavinōdanallūr.

An important royal official who had made considerable endowments to the temple at Tiruvarur belonged to a distinguished line of Pallavarayas, who served successive Cola monarchs, like Rajaraja II, Rajadhiraja II and Kulottunga III. This Pallavarayan served under Rajadhiraja II. The large village, Ammaiappanallur, which lies 4 miles west of Tiruvarur, was given tax-free to this Pallavarayan by the King Rajaraja II. He, in turn, granted the entire village, which was his *kāni*, by paying the tax dues for 1500 *kāśus.*[10] Besides his own village, this official made other grants of land too. Yet another record refers to a grant of land by a member of a regiment, called Tyāgavalli Velaikkārar, after buying and making it tax-free on the payment of 26 *kāśus* to the *sabhā* of Vāyarrūr.[11]

As in the case of the royal temple, top royal officials have contributed to the temple at Tiruvarur. But here, they do not seem to be under any obligation to do so. On the other hand, the important officials assumed the mantle of patrons of non-royal temples and lavished their wealth on them. It is more likely that they did so as an act of piety and not out of any compulsion.

As mentioned earlier, most of the land grants were situated within a radius of 12 miles from Tiruvarur. The only exception seems to be a land grant by Kulottunga III.[12] In an insc. from Seranur and Kudumiyamalai, he claims to have distributed the tribute of gold and tax-free lands levied from the country of the Ceras and the Pandyas among the temples of Chidambaram, Tiruvarur and Tribhuvanam.

Even in the post-Cola period, private endowments have been recorded. The first non-Cola record belongs to the 40th year of Maravarman Kulasekharadeva.[13] It refers to a land grant by an individual. Similarly, another

Pandyan record[14] refers to a land grant by an individual for conducting *vēda adhyayanam.* There are instances of land grants during the Nayakar rule, too. So we see, there are many grants[15] for various services instituted by successive dynasties. The property and wealth of the temple has kept growing over the centuries by the acts of piety of kings and commoners.

The yield per acre of land is not stated. Nor is it mentioned whether the lands granted were one-crop lands (*oruppū-nilam*) or two-crop lands (*iruppū-nilam*). Therefore, it is not clear whether any uniformity in making land grants was followed, by which one could calculate the yield and therefore, the revenue. However, since all the land that was granted was in and around the Tiruvarur area, which lies in the delta region of the Kaveri, it can be safely deduced that the lands were all high-yielding, fertile tracts. If we go by the standard yield of 100 *kalams* of paddy per *vēli* of land, we can calculate roughly the income in paddy which was due to the temple. But many of the inscs. do not give us this vital information of the area granted. So we have to content ourselves with the location of the lands.

CASH INVESTMENTS

Generally, the endowments in cash and gold were made by the kings and their retinue, who had vast resources of wealth at their command. In the *bhakti* temples, most of the endowments were made by individuals and not by kings. Thus we see that many of the grants were land grants and very few endowments mention cash or gold. This is in sharp contrast to grants to the royal temples like the Rajarajesvaram, where cash or gold was granted for making many endowments for lamps. It could mean that circulation of cash was limited.

An insc. of the 32nd year of Parantaka I[16] states that the *sabhā* of Pandanainallur, a *brahmadēya* in Tiruvarur-Kurram, undertook to provide oil for a lamp, out of the interest accruing from a donation of 30 *kalañju* gold granted by *Śrikōyil Dēvanār.* This early Cola record is an instance of money being invested with the village *sabhā,* which agreed to pay the interest in the form of oil for lamps.

Yet another record[17] says that a gold deposit was made by a Vilupparaiyan of Purakkudi in Ambar nāḍu. This was entrusted with the merchants of Tiruvarur for providing offerings for oil for bath as well as gifts of gold for clothes for the images and fees for the temple songsters and servants.

This is an investment made with the merchants who agreed to pay the interest which was utilised for the above-mentioned purposes.

The temple treasury (*paṇḍāram*) lent 200 *kalañju*, deposited by Sembiyam Madevi (for food offerings), to the village assembly of Adiyappiya CVM.[18]

In this manner the temple treasury redistributed money to village assemblies, individuals and groups. It maintained records in the '*paṇḍārappottagam*'. The temple treasury was also referred to as *Tyāgavinōdan Paṇḍāram*.

LOCAL BODIES AND THE TEMPLE

The *bhakti* temple was managed for the most part by the local bodies and groups in conjunction with the temple administration. The royal government rarely interfered in its day-to-day administration and only stepped in to sort out cases of conflict or litigation. The *sabhās* of the surrounding villages played an active role in managing the temple and its endowments.

Executing Endowments

As mentioned earlier, right from the earliest recorded insc. belonging to the time of Aditya I,[19] the *ūravar* of Tiruvarur agreed to implement endowments. A similar undertaking was made by the *sabhā* of Pandanainallur in Tiruvarur-Kurram[20] to provide oil for a lamp out of the interest from 30 *kalanju* gold donated by the *Srīkōyil-Dēvanār*.

The lands which were gifted to the temple were usually taken care of by the donors. An individual of Kalanivayil of Eyil-nāḍu granted some land in Sirunallur, a *brahmadēya* in Tevur-nāḍu as *tirunāmattukkāni*. This land was purchased in the 32nd year of Maravarman Kulasekhara Pandya, but enjoyed by the donor himself. He made the grant 8 years later.[21] At times, the land was given to a third party for cultivation on the condition that they hand over the produce or interest (*poli*) to the temple. Elsewhere, the *sabhās* executed the endowments themselves.

Apart from assemblies, we have seen how groups of people, like *Śivabrāhmanas*[22] and merchants,[23] also involved themselves in managing endowments. In this manner the strain of administering endowments was removed from the temple administrative body. All that the temple administration had to do was to monitor the endowments. This, as already noted, was done by the temple treasury.

Individual donors paid specific sums to the village assemblies for getting their endowments exempted from taxes. The stipulated amount was paid into the temple treasury, which, in turn, transferred it to the governing bodies.[24]

Similarly, the members of the *mahāsabhā* of Tirunallur came to Tiruvarur and assembling at the *Dēvāśriyan-mandapam,* exempted a piece of gifted land in their village from taxes. They declared that they made the grant on behalf of an individual from whom they had received 100 *kāśus.*[25] The *nagarattār* of Tiruvarur are mentioned in a sale of land to the temple, made in the reign of Kulottunga I.[26]

We see, thus, that most of the endowments were made by individuals (usually from nearby areas) and managed by local bodies, temple managers and even by individuals.

ROYAL INVOLVEMENT

The involvement of the royal house in the affairs of the Tiruvarur Temple took the form of endowments in gold and land; in making *kāni* grants to temple authorities; in making renovations and extensions to the temple complex; and occasionally interceding in administrative matters like settling disputes. The role of the kings and their royal retinue in the temple was primarily that of leading devotees. As ardent Saivites, the Colas patronised the leading Siva temples of the land, especially the ones which had a hoary tradition and association with the *bhakti* saints.

The grand old lady of the Cola house, Sembiyam Madevi, is credited with building several Siva temples in the Tanjavur region, as well as with rebuilding many existing temples in stone. The earliest record of royal patronage belongs to the 2nd year of Rajaraja I.[27] It refers to a grant of silver vessels by Sembiyam Madevi for the merit of Uttama Cola. In the 7th year of Rajaraja,[28] the same lady set up two idols of Sundarar and his consort, and presented 234 *kasus* as *pudukkupuram*[29] (capital funds for renovation). Provisions were also made for worship and for offerings. Another record[30] refers to the Acalesvara shrine being rebuilt in stone by the same royal patroness.

The benefactions of Anukkiyar Paravai Nangaiyar, the courtesan, have been mentioned earlier. She is said to have donated as much as 20,643 *kalañju* of gold and plated the doors of the shrine and the pillars of the *mandapam* with 42,000 *palams* of copper.

In the reign of Rajendra II,[31] a royal order was issued to cover with gold plate certain portions of the sanctum and the *ardhamandapa* of the temple. Kulottunga III claims to have built the massive *gōpura* of Valmikadhipati, according to an insc. found at his royal temple of Kampaharesvara at Tribhuvanam.[32]

Among the significant land grants made by the kings is the one by Kulottunga II.[33] Kulottunga III[34] has also made land grants to this temple. (These grants are mentioned in the section on Land Grants.)

DISPUTES

Among the administrative orders of the kings, one belongs to Rajadhiraja II.[35] This order restored to the temple servants house sites formerly granted to them by Vikrama Cola, after making allotments for merchants (*cheṭṭis*), oil-mongers (*chekkars*), their followers and guards—Cholendrasingan *Velaikkarar*. These sites were encroached upon by the *cheṭṭis* for their dwellings and shops. After evicting the *cheṭṭis*, a compensation of 100 *kāśus* was paid to the temple servants. The order was conveyed at the instance of the important Cola officer called Pallavarayan Vedavanamudaiya Ammaiyappan.

Similarly, Kulottunga III[36] interfered in a dispute among temple servants (*ānḍars*) who had failed to distribute properly amongst themselves the lands previously allotted to them; and in quarrelling, they left their lands uncultivated. So, the king ordered the redistribution of tax-free lands among the 100 *ānḍars* at the request of his officers, a Pallavaraiyan and a royal officer (*tirumandirāolai*). Yet another royal order,[37] this time belonging to Vikrama Cola, restored a place-site to Palaiyurudaiyan Candrasekhara, said to be a descendant of the minister of Manuniti Cola, the legendary Cola ancestor.

SECULAR ADMINISTRATION

Among the temple functionaries who looked after the secular affairs of the temple, were the *Śrikāryam* Officer, the Devakanmis, the Supervisor(s), the Accountants and the Treasurers. No mention is found in the records of *Sthānattārs* or the Joint Trustees.

Dēvakanmis: They were the executive officers who received the endowments.

Śrīkāryam: In the Tiruvarur Temple, the *Śrīkāryam* officers were important local men. For instance, in the reign of Rajaraja I,[38] *Sembiyan-ambar-*

nāṭṭu-kōṇar was the *Śrīkāryam.* In the reign of Rajendra I,[39] the *Śrīkāryam* was a high-ranking officer, *Solavijaya(dya)dhara MVN* of Inganāḍu. During the reign of Kulottunga III,[40] the *Śrīkāryam* was *Pungudaiyan Vira-vichchadira* (*Vidyadhara*) *Pallavaraiyan,* who granted lands as *antarayankollaurkkil iraiyili* for daily food offerings to the Vinayakar deity, set up by the donor himself. Tiruvarur was one of the five secondary capitals of the Colas. Therefore, the temple at Tiruvarur would have been considered important enough to have high officials appointed to important positions in its administration.

Ponnuswamy[41] is of the opinion that the *Śrīkāryam* was connected more with the religious side of the administration. However, in the light of the above-mentioned inscs., it is clear that the *Śrīkāryam* was held by landed gentry and high officials like *Mūvēndavēlāns* and *Pallavaraiyans.* Therefore, it is unlikely that the *Śrīkāryam* looked after the religious side of the administration alone.

As to the manner of appointing the *Śrīkāryam* officer, no mention is made anywhere of the procedure to be followed. It is unlikely that these appointments should have been made by the royal government. In all probability, the *Śrīkāryam* officer was chosen from the landed gentry of nearby villages of Tiruvarur. Persons of economic and social status and devotion seem to have been chosen. The post was not hereditary.

Accountant : The *Kōil-kaṇakku* or accountant is mentioned in many inscs. Among them was the Head Accountant (*mudal-kaṇakku*). A record of the 40th year of Maravarman Kulasekhara Pandya[42] mentions the *Kōil-Mudal-Karnattār.* The elaborate royal order belonging to Kulottunga II[43] gives the names of several temple functionaries. Among them are a few accountants.

The method of their remuneration is not clear. However, one record[44] does state that a *kōil-kaṇakku* was paid 3 portions of paddy plus one *kāśu;* while another was paid 4 portions of paddy plus *kāśu.* The reasons for this ambiguity are not clear.

The *kōil-kaṇakku* or *karnattār* kept temple accounts, as in other temples. The income of such a large temple as the Tyagarajasvami must have been considerable. Therefore, this was an important temple post held by responsible local people. There is no mention of any particular group, like the weavers, who were entrusted with the accountancy work of the temple. Mention is found of an *Ārāyci.*[45] This person's name was Munaippadi Udaiyan, therefore, a local chief. Ponnuswamy[46] feels that he was a person who managed temple properties or checked temple accounts (an auditor).

Treasurers: The temple treasury was also called *Tyāgavinōda Bhandāram.*[47] It maintained its own records in the *Bhanḍārappottagam.*[48] The treasurer was referred to as the *kōyil samudāyam.* Grants were made in the presence of village officials and temple officers like the *mudal-kaṇakku* and the *kōil-samudāyam.*[49]

Most temples had at least two treasuries—one for cash and gold, and another for temple jewels. Tiruvarur had enormous quantities of precious stones and precious metals like gold and silver. The jewel chests were called the *poṇbhanḍaram.* It received gifts of gold ornaments made by several people, like the one made by a person from Pundi.[50] Similarly, a gift of a wreath of precious stones, made by a person from Gangaikondasolapuram, would have been kept in the gold-treasury.[51]

An undated record[52] states that the jewel chests, which were in the custody of one individual, were now in the joint charge of two officers, *Brahmamārāyan* and *Viluppparayan.* It delineates the steps to be taken, if the seals of the treasury-room were mishandled. In several temples, the jewel room could only be entered jointly by two or three stipulated individuals or *bhaṭṭars* (often wearing no more than a loin-cloth). This was to check embezzlement or theft and ensured a sharing of responsibility.

Supervisors: There were supervisors for various duties. A temple supervisor or overseer, *Kōil-kankāṇiseyvār,* is mentioned in the Pandyan record of Maravarman Kulasekhara Pandyan.[53]

SPIRITUAL FUNCTIONARIES

Māhēśvaras: These authorities in Saiva *āgamas* were also involved in temple administration. The varied role of the *māhēśvaras,* in not only royal temples and *maṭhas,* but in almost all Saiva temples, has been described (vide Chapter II). An insc.[54] of the time of Kulottunga I refers to an endowment for offerings on specified occasions for feeding *Sivayōgins* and *Māhēśvaras.* An order of Kulottunga III[55] was addressed to *devakanmis, māhēśvara kankāni* and *śrīkāryam.* The *māhēśvara kankāni* was the overseer/supervisor/head of the spiritual *māhēśvaras.*

Arcakas: They were the priests who performed the actual *pūjā.* The long royal order of Kulottunga II[56] refers to several temple functionaries. It mentions an *arcaka,* who was paid three portions of paddy plus 3 *kāśus.* One *archanaipannuvār* (literally meaning one who does the *arcana*) was paid 3 3/16 portions paddy plus one cloth and 3 *kāśus*. It also mentions 3 numbers *Tiruparicārakas* who were paid 1 3/16 portions of paddy plus one *kāśu*.

QUASI-RELIGIOUS FUNCTIONARIES

Dēvaradiyār: The *devaradiyār* or dancing girls were attached to most temples. The Tiruvarur Temple in particular had a hoary tradition of dancing girls. It is here that Sundarar married Paravai Nacciyar, the temple dancer, who is mentioned in the *Periyapuranam*. Sembiyam Madevi[57] set up two idols of the saint and his consort, Paravai Nacciyar, and donated 234 *kāśus* for daily services to these images. This shows the antiquity of the system of temple dancers and the high esteem they commanded.

The title of *Talai Kōḷi* was assumed by a *dēvadāsi*.[58] This title had been conferred on Madhavi by the king in *Silappadikāram*.[59] In the Tiruvarur Temple we find several epigraphical references to endowments made by Anukkiyar Paravai Nangaiyar, who is referred to as a *nakkan̲* in the record of Rajadhiraja I.[60] *Nakkan̲* means an accomplished dancing girl, according to the Tamil lexicon.[61] Paravai Nangaiyar was a great favourite of Rajendra I. She shared the temple honours with him. Rajendra had a temple and a village named after her as Paravai Isvarar and Paravaipuram respectively.[62]

The dancing girls were well-remunerated. As pointed out in the section on the *dēvaradiyār* in the Tanjavur Temple, each dancer was granted a house, 100 *kalams* paddy etc. Among them, some, who became important temple dancers, or who became favourites of kings and landed gentry, had vast incomes at their command. The grants in cash and gold made by Paravai Nangaiyar had been mentioned earlier in this chapter. A record belonging to the reign of Rajendra III[63] states that a land grant was made by purchasing the land from a dancing girl (*paḍiyilar*), called Umaiyalvi.

The temple town of Tiruvarur supplied more than 50 dancing girls to the royal temple of Rajarajesvaram. Of these, the contribution of the Tyagarajasvami Temple was itself quite considerable. Therefore, it follows that the institution of *dēvaradiyārs* was very ancient and well-established in Tiruvarur. They were recruited from the surrounding villages or the town of Tiruvarur itself. Since these posts were generally hereditary, most of the dancing girls must have belonged to Tiruvarur and its environs.

Nivendakkārar: Among the several temple staff were musicians, gardeners, potters, washermen, etc. The long insc. of Kulottunga II[64] mentions torch-bearers, cooks, garland-makers, servants mixing incense, servants gathering flowers, servants supplying firewood to the temple kitchen, women cleaning rice, conch-blowers, trumpeteers, servants carrying the deity in procession, potters, barbers, etc. (for example the insc. mentions, among others, *tirumandapaalu nandavana tirupalli tonganendutu, madaipaḻḻi kośavar, tiruparisāttanvanattār,* etc.).

Grants were made to support the singers in the temple. A record[65] mentions a gold deposit made with the merchants of Tiruvarur for among other things fees for temple musicians and servants. Another grant of land[66] in Vayarrur was made to Pungoyil *nambi* (who composed the *Viranukka-vijayam* in honour of Virasola-*anukkar*). This person was probably a composer of a drama in honour of the *Anukkar*—perhaps groups of persons immediately attending on the king (a group of warriors). Land grants[67] were also made for paying two servants bringing water from the nearby river for the holy bath; for servants working in the garden in Uttamasolamangalam in Panaiyurnāḍu; and servants supplying hay for the cows (*gōśālaisurabhigaḷ*), etc. Kani grants were made for *parichārakas,* and others like the drama master mentioned above, by important officers like the *Ghaṭika-Maharaja,* who acted as the *kēḻvi.*[68]

A record of Kulottunga III[69] mentions the redistribution of tax-free land to 100 *āṇḍār,* as mentioned earlier. A similar record (mentioned earlier) mentions house-sites granted to temple servants. These *kāni* grants were made by the villagers/*sabhās* to the various artisans and servants for their contribution and services to the temple. They were not always royal grants.

LOCALISED NATURE OF THE TEMPLE

The Tiruvarur Temple was a locally-controlled and independently-administered temple. The royal government's role has been restricted to making endowments and interceding in long standing conflicts. Beyond that, there is very little evidence of interference from the royal government.

Appointments: Most of the personnel employed in the temple were recruited locally. Even the *śrīkāryam* officer belonged to the landed gentry from nearby villages of *nāḍus,* like Inganāḍu. The inscs. do not state clearly as to the manner of appointment of the temple staff.

Redistribution: As to the redistribution of resources, much of the grants for lamps were entrusted with local bodies, who undertook to provide the requisite oil for the temple. The *sabhā* of Pandanainallur-kurram[70] (very close to Tiruvarur) undertook to provide oil for a lamp out of the interest from 30 *kalañju* of gold deposited by an individual. It does not state whether the *sabhā* chose shepherds from outside their village. In the event of an endowment being received by a local body or by an individual or by groups, it is more likely that they would have looked after the implementation themselves, in order to ensure that the money was utilised for the development of the community concerned.

Endowments from the military sector were few as compared with such temples as Tiruvidaimarudur, which were managed almost entirely by military regiments. In the case of the Rajarajesvaram too, several shrines were maintained by regiments. The *sabhā* of Vayarrur,[71] a *brahmadēya* in Tiruvarur-kurram, received 26 *kāśus* out of the amount endowed to the temple by a member of a regiment called Tyagavalli Velaikkarar.

As already stated, the villages lying within a radius of 12 miles from Tiruvarur were closely associated with this temple, which formed the focal point of that area. This is to a lesser degree what the Rajarajesvaram was to the entire region of Colamandalam.

Thus we see how Tiruvarur evolved over the centuries from humble beginnings and grew in size and importance to become the focal point of Tiruvarur-kurram. This, as we have noted, was primarily due to local involvement in the affairs of the temple. It was the nucleus of the locality; it was administered by the people of the locality and it has received its sustenance primarily due to its holy associations. That is why it still continues to be an important Saiva place of pilgrimage, and festivals, which began even before Appar's time, still continue uninterrupted to this date.

The fact that such a large temple as Tiruvarur, with a staff of hundreds (and which sent several temple functionaries, including many dancing girls to the Rajarajesvaram), could be managed and developed on the funds at its disposal, gives the lie to the need for the huge wealth in land and gold for managing the royal temple of Tanjavur. It is true that the Rajarajesvaram had the biggest temple body; but large-sized *bhakti* temples like Tiruvarur, too, had a considerably large temple *parivāram*. Thus, to manage and administer such a temple as the Rajarajesvaram, there was no necessity for such enormous funds. However, if the king had wished to use the royal temple as an instrument of extending and establishing Cola hegemony, then we can understand why such vast resources in land and gold were lavished on royal temples.

REFERENCES

1. Sambandar, 4:101:6.
2. Ponnuswamy, Sri Thyagaraja Temple—Tiruvarur, Ch. II.
3. S.R. Balasubramanyam, Early Chola Temples, pp. 192-197.
4. SII, VII, 485.
5. S.R. Balasubramanyam, Middle Chola Temples, p. 275.
6. 190, 191, 192 of 1907.
7. SII, XIII, 291.
8. 679 of 1991.
9. SII, VII, 485.
10. SII, VII, 587.
11. SII, VII, 607.
12. Insc. of Pudukottai State, Nos. 163 & 166.
13. 551 of 1904; SII, XVII, 596.
14. 589 of 1904; SII, XVII, 584.
15. 536 of 1904; SII, XVII, 581.
16. SII, XVII, 619.
17. 678 of 1919.
18. 680 of 1919.
19. SII, XIII, 291.
20. SII, XVII, 619.
21. SII, XVII, 596.
22. 556 of 1904; SII, XVII, 601.
23. 678 of 1919.
24. 677 of 1919; SII, XVII, 608, 609.
25. 564 of 1904; SII, XVII, 609.
26. SII, XVII, 578.
27. 570 of 1904; SII, XIII, 1.
28. 571 of 1904; SII, XVII, 617.
29. Ibid.
30. 572 of 1904; SII, XIII, 291.
31. 675 of 1919.
32. 190, 191, 192 of 1907.
33. 291 of 1901; SII, VII, 485.
34. Insc. of Pud. St., 163 & 166.
35. 543 of 1904; SII, XVII, 588.
36. SII, XVII, 599.
37. SII, V, 455.
38. SII, XVII, 617.
39. SII, XVII, 613.
40. SII, XVII, 595.
41. Ponnuswamy, op. cit., Ch. V.

42. SII, XVII, 596.
43. SII, VII, 485.
44. Ibid.
45. SII, XIII, 291.
46. Ponnuswamy, op. cit.
47. SII, XVII, 586.
48. 672 of 1919.
49. SII, XVII, 584.
50. 670 of 1919.
51. 676 of 1919.
52. 681 of 1919.
53. SII, XVII, 596.
54. SII, XVII, 625.
55. Pud. Insc., 163.
56. SII, VII, 485.
57. 571 of 1904; SII, XVII, 617.
58. SII, XVII, 606.
59. III, II, 318-20.
60. 679 of 1919.
61. Tamil Lexicon, Vol. IV, pp. 21-22.
62. 317 of 1917.
63. SII, XVII, 600.
64. SII, VII, 485.
65. 678 of 1919.
66. SII, XVII, 593.
67. SII, XVII, 597.
68. SII, XVII, 591.
69. SII, XVII, 599.
70. SII, XVII, 619.
71. SII, XVII, 609.

Chapter IV

CONCLUSIONS

This thesis identifies two kinds of temples—royal and *bhakti* and brings out the differences between them. It further highlights the role of the royal temple of Tanjavur in establishing and consolidating Cola power. The study of the royal temple of Rajarajesvaram highlights the importance of the temple as a royal institution and shows the power wielded by the Cola government through the temple. This is the rationale behind the manner in which this royal temple's activities and special features have been divided and analysed under different sections.

The thesis studies certain other temples from the same angle. This is to show how *bhakti* temples differed from royal temples as religious institutions and how they lacked the requisite influence/control over vast areas as did their royal counterparts. It helps to emphasise the limited constituencies of these temples vis-a-vis those of the royal temples.

The analysis of pre-Rajaraja temples belonging to the Pallava period helps to show the royal temple as an institution of royal power in its incipient or nascent stage. This contrasts with the royal temple of Rajaraja's time and highlights the maturity and influence gained by it in the middle Cola period.

TWO KINDS OF TEMPLES—BHAKTI AND ROYAL

a) The *bhakti* temples (and the non-royal temples) trace their origin to an emotion or faith. They originated as small shrines (for the most part) usually built of perishable material. Due to their association with the *bhakti* saints, these temples attracted benefactions from kings and laymen alike. This, in turn, led to their gradual growth from small, modest shrines to large temple complexes. The patronage to *bhakti* temples cut across dynastic lines, with the kings of succeeding dynasties adding to the growth and development of the temple as an architectural entity and as a religious institution. Several services and festivals were initiated and maintained by people belonging to different periods, which continue almost uninterrupted to this day. Thus, we can trace the growth of the temple through the architectural and sculptural styles of different dynasties. The *bhakti* temples are 'living' temples where service initiated more than a thousand years ago continues till modern times. All these characteristics of *bhakti* temples have been discussed and elaborated upon in the chapter on the *bhakti* temple of Tiruvarur.

The royal temples (as classified in this thesis) were temples built by monarchs to their chosen gods. The sculptural themes in the royal temples reflected the monarchs' preference for a particular cult. It did not have much to do with current popular beliefs. The projection of the Somaskanda cult by the Pallavas is a moot point. In their own royal constructions, they could introduce their chosen cults and practices as well as promote *maṭhas* of their choice. The construction of these temples was paid for by the kings themselves (either from their own wealth or from war booty or perhaps from levies on the public). They were one-time constructions, generally completed in the lifetime of their builders.

b) The *bhakti* temples originated as small structures, built usually of brick and mortar. A few of them were grand structures built by kings (like the Vaikunta Perumal Temple of Kanci), but most of them were local temples built by the community. As such, they lacked the grandeur in conception and execution of their royal counterparts. They acquired grandeur as they gained in importance.

The royal temples were grand in design and execution. The royal temples built by the Pallavas were majestic edifices, built in stone (a medium not in common use), and truly awe-inspiring to their subjects. The skill required to build these magnificent temples could have only been got together by monarchs with considrable power and wealth at their disposal.

Vimānas were the most important architectural components of the temple complexes till the end of the Cola period. The *gōpuras* or gateways, in contrast, grew in height only in the post-Cola period. Therefore, all the tall *vimānas* of temples belong to the Cola or pre-Cola period. The *vimānas* of the royal temples are among the tallest structures of the medieval period. In comparison, no *bhakti* temple could boast of such tall *vimānas.*

H. Sarkar, in his book on *The Kampaharesvara Temple at Tribhuvanam,* has given a table giving the comparative heights of some temples in South India. Of the temples analysed, those that were built by monarchs (i.e. royal temples) have the tallest structures. The total heights of some of the temples are given in Table 10.

TABLE 10

Sl. No.	Name of Place	Name of Temple	Total Height
a)	Darasuram	Airavatesvara Temple	83' (25.26 m)
b)	Gangaikondacolapuram	Gangaikondacolisvara Temple	180' (54.86 m)
c)	Kancipuram	Kailasanatha Temple	66.33' (20.27 m)
d)	Mahabalipuram	Shore Temple	55.42' (16.96 m)
e)	Kancipuram	Vaikunta Perumal Temple	72.75' (22.06 m)
f)	Pattadakal	Virupaksha Temple	61' (18.59 m)
g)	Tanjavur	Brihadisvara Temple	196.50' (59.98 m)
h)	Tribhuvanam	Kampaharesvara Temple	126' (38.40 m)
i)	Uttaramerur	Sundaravarada Perumal Temple	59' (17.98 m)

These are the tallest temples in the South. Almost all of them are royal constructions. It is seen how the *vimānas* of Cola and pre-Cola royal temples towered over those of *bhakti* temples. The royal temple of Rajarajesvaram (Brihadisvara Temple) is the tallest at a majestic height of 196.50'. All the four Cola royal temples have very tall *vimānas*; the Darasuram Temple being the shortest at 83'. Even the pre-Cola royal temples have tall structures. The earliest structural temple of the Pallavas at Mahabalipuram had a fairly tall *vimāna*. Though the Vaikunta Perumal Temple at Kanci is classified as a *bhakti* temple, it is very much a royal construction, having been built by Nandivarman II. Even the Calukyan royal temple of Pattadakal has a tall *vimāna*.

One of the reasons for this distinction in heights between the two types of temples could be attributed to the nature of patronage of the temples concerned. The *bhakti* temples on being rebuilt in stone would have had their *vimānas* consecrated. Once consecrated, the structure would not have been interfered with. The patronage of the *bhakti* temples grew over a period of time. Consequently, their structures also grew in size. On the other hand, the royal temple was planned at the outset as a grand monument. The size and height of the superstructures and *vimanas* would have been planned before the start of construction.

c) The *bhakti* temples are dynamic institutions. Starting as modest shrines, they acquired sanctity by their association with the *bhakti* saints—the *nāyanārs* and the *ālvārs*. This, in turn, attracted benefactions from kings and commoners alike, who made additions to their complexes. The monarchs and royal retinues of each dynasty added to the growth and the development of the temples architecturally and initiated additional services and festivals. Thus, we can trace the growth of the temple complex from the architectural and sculptural styles of various dynasties incorporated into the structure of the temples.

The royal temples were built completely in the form visualised by their builders. Very few additional constructions were seen in later times. It is for this reason that most of them were incomplete to some extent for, after the demise of their creators, the successors turned their attention to their own temples (as in the case of the Rajarajesvaram). It is a sorry sight to find these grand architectural monuments of immense beauty incomplete in one form or other.

d) The *bhakti* temples attracted the patronage of kings and laymen (as stated earlier). Herein, the kings were the devotees of the deities of the temples. They did not seek to impose their chosen preferences on the sculptural themes of the temples or on the forms of worship in practice. However, it is true that the monarchs chose to patronise only their chosen gods and were niggardly in their patronage to the rival streams. For instance, the Colas openly patronised the major and minor Siva temples but did not take the initiative to construct any major Visnu temple comparable to the Rajarajesvaram or the Gangaikondacolisvaram. By contrast, the Vijayanagara dynasty extended greater support to Vaisnava temples. Several Vaisnava centres came up during their rule.

The Imperial Colas built temples only to Siva, as Siva was their patron deity. Rajasimha, the Pallava king, was also parochial in his support to Saivism. His successor, Nandivarman II, was an ardent Vaisnavite. This is seen in his royal temple to Visnu, the Vaikunta Perumal Temple of Kanci. The early temples of Uttaramerur, a *brahmadēya* which was established during the reign of this monarch, are also dedicated to Visnu, viz. the Sundaravarada Perumal Temple, the Vaikunta Perumal Temple, the Govardhana Temple etc.

e) The administration of most non-royal temples including *bhakti* temples was vested with local bodies. When they were of modest size, they were managed by the local *sabhās* through a special committee for temple affairs. As the temples and their services grew in size, the *sabhās* found themselves unequal to the task of managing their affairs. So a separate temple administrative body was created which consisted of prominent members of the locality. The day-to-day administration was in the hands of full-time executive officers, accountants, treasurers, and other functionaries. This body grew in size depending on the importance gained by the temple. The administration of these temples was not at any time under the government's control for it was not a creation of the government. It was the local bodies who had a say in the temple matters. We have seen how these temple bodies outgrew the importance of the local assemblies and in due course, became more powerful than the latter.

The administrative machinery of the royal temples was created by the government. The administration of these temples was more streamlined with the division of responsibilities on a rational basis. This can be attributed to the creation of a full-fledged administrative body for the temple. Here, the responsibilities and powers were well-delineated without ambiguity. The large temple body was used to administer grants and monitor services to the temple. Several of these grants were located in far-off places. The royal temple could manage these grants because the temple administrative body could get the support of the other government agencies too, for instance, the army.

f) The benefactions attracted by *bhakti* temples from kings and commoners contributed to their wealth. The royal officers, both of the bureaucracy and from the military, actively involved themselves in the affairs of the *bhakti* temples. But here, their involvement seems to have been out of a voluntary will and not out of compulsion from ruling monarchs. The wealth at the command of these temples was quite substantial. Grants of land, cash and gold were made for maintaining services and festivals and for remunerating the temple staff. However, the wealth of even large-sized *bhakti* temples, like Tiruvarur, did not compare with the wealth of royal temples like the Rajarajesvaram of Rajaraja.

The royal temples had considerable resources. This, as already stated, was because kings lavished their wealth (from wars, etc.) on their temples. Apart from this, royal officers, landed gentry and military officers were obliged to patronise the royal temples. It is quite likely that there was an obligatory commitment to associate themselves with the royal temples.

g) The limited wealth or resources at the command of the *bhakti* temples, in turn, were responsible for restricting the constituencies of these temples to the region of their origin and its immediate neighbourhood. The villages mentioned in the records of Tiruvarur cover an overall area of 12 miles or so. Therefore, the effective area of influence of this temple was confined to its immediate environs. Important *bhakti* temples did attract benefactions from pilgrims; but save a few like Tirupati, Chidambaram and Srirangam, most *bhakti* temples sustained their activities only from local contributions and involvement. The kings and their retinue were devotees of *bhakti* temples; however, the administration of the latter could not depend upon governmental assistance in managing their properties and other affairs. With limited power, the *bhakti* temples had small constituencies as compared to the entire Cola empire which was under the influence of the Rajarajesvaram.

The power of the monarchs was instrumental in enlarging the constituencies of their royal undertakings well beyond their immediate neighbourhood. The influence of the Rajarajesvaram of Tanjavur was spread over the entire Tamil country and included the conquered territories of Andhra, Mysore, Kerala and Ilam. This was possible because powerful monarchs could command the services of their officers for the benefit of their temples.

h) Most *bhakti* temples were the nuclei of temple towns. That is to say, village settlements around these temples grew in size and became temple towns. These small hamlets grew into large settlements due to the fame and sanctity acquired by the temples through their association with the *bhakti* saints. The towns acquired sanctity due to these temples.

The royal temple, on the other hand, was often built to sanctify a royal centre or a new capital. The Pallava and Cola kings built grand temples with the prime motive of sanctifying their cities.

i) The land grants to the non-royal or *bhakti* temples mention the lumpsum tax which was paid to make them tax-free. This was known as *pūrvacāram* in the Pallava records and as *iṛai-dravyam* in Cola times. All land grants to temples in pre-Cola and Cola times mention this tax.

However, the land grants which were made to the royal temple of Rajarajesvaram do not mention this tax. The insc. simply states that Rajaraja gave the villages as *dēvadāna* to the royal temple for expenses of the temple. The supreme authority and power of the Cola monarch is evident in transferring in an *ad-hoc* manner the land revenue from several villages to the royal temple.

j) Finally, a study of the life-span of the two types of temples shows the crucial difference in their nature. Royal temples had a limited life-span (as has been seen in all the case-studies made in this thesis). Most of them ceased to grow in size as a complex after the demise of the kings who built them. Their importance dwindled and active service in many of them stopped within a short time.

This is in contrast to the continuity in service in *bhakti* temples. Not dependent on the patronage of kings alone, these temples drew their sustenance from the common man's largesse. It is the common man who has kept these temples alive through his acts of voluntary faith, thus driving home the truth that grandeur in design is no substitute for sanctity.

THE ROYAL TEMPLE UNDER RAJARAJA

The chapters on the Pallava royal temple of Rajasimha (the Kailasanatha Temple of Kanci) and the Cola royai temple of Rajaraja (the Brihadisvara Temple of Tanjavur) show to what extent the royal temple evolved as an institution of royal power, under the Middle Colas. The Pallava temple was a grand, royal monument—a symbol of the Pallava king's religious sentiments and a manifestation of the royal person. It did not seem to extend its influence over the Pallava domain in the way the Tanjavur temple achieved almost three hundred years later.

In contrast, not only did Rajaraja build a magnificent monument worthy of the mightiest of the Southern monarchs, but he gave it the power and wealth to command allegiance from all parts of his empire. It was he who used the royal temple to consolidate imperial Cola power over the conquered territories. This he achieved by granting villages from these regions as *dēvadānas* to the temple. He thus created a liaison between the royal temple in the capital city of Tanjavur and the outlying provinces (*puramandalam*). Rajaraja used the religious medium of the temple to act as the consolidating force. Religion had a powerful appeal and he translated this appeal into an institution, which influenced and controlled (albeit indirectly) various regions—both in the core region of Colamandalam and the conquered territories.

The administration of the royal temple of Tanjavur was done by the largest body of temple functionaries, with well-delineated powers and responsibilities. These personnel were appointed directly by the government. The vast properties of this royal temple required such a large, well-oiled administrative body, and only a monarch of the prestige of Rajaraja could command the services of personnel from far-off areas. In the appointment of temple functionaries is seen the autocratic authority of the Cola monarch.

The royal temple enjoyed revenue from as many as 40 villages of Colamandalam granted to it as *dēvadāna.* This was apart from the 16 or so villages from the outer provinces. No other temple had property, gold and cash as much as this royal temple did. It has been seen (in the Ch. on Tiruvarur) that a large temple does not really require such huge resources to manage its affairs. Therefore, it is clear that Rajaraja wished to link every part of his empire to his temple in some form or other either through land grants or through lamp grants or through the appointment of personnel. He had to make the royal temple a mighty institution worthy of being associated with by his subjects. In this way he made his royal temple a symbol of his great empire.

The Cola kings were ardent Saivites and this has been seen in their patronage to Siva temples. Rajaraja and his successors used the medium of the royal temple to promote Saiva beliefs, myths and cults. New sculptural themes were introduced glorifying Siva and highlighting Siva's superior status over Visnu and the other gods. The Cola monarchs extended their patronage to leading Siva temples of the Tamil country, particularly to Chidambaram; but it was mainly through their royal institutions that they could project their affiliation to their chosen cults and beliefs. Here, they were influenced by the royal *gurus* (particularly of the Golaki *maṭha*).

They encouraged worship in strict accordance with the *āgamic* prescriptions. By extending state patronage to Saivism in various ways, like institutionalising the *Tēvaram* hymns, building great temples to Siva and establishing the worship of the *liṅga* in all Siva temples, the Cola kings, after Rajaraja, managed to project themselves as champions of Saivism. Rajaraja built the most magnificent temple to Siva in his capital, thus elevating Siva to the position of the Supreme Deity. Saivism was glorified, often at the expense of Vaisnavism.

The ritual control of the royal temple extended over the Cola bureaucracy and military. Top-ranking officers were obliged to be associated with the royal institution in several ways (as discussed in the relevant sections on the Rajarajesvaram). The association of Cola ranked groupings with the royal temple was an ingenious way of establishing the position of the monarch as the ritual head of society. The institution of the royal temple was used to project the Cola king as the foremost *bhakta* of his chosen god, Siva, and in this manner gain legitimacy from his subjects.

Rajaraja and his successors attempted to project their own glory through the institution of the royal temples that they built. This they achieved through several methods. By naming the deity of the temple after themselves (for example the Rajarajesvaram) and by installing massive *liṅgas* in majestic, architectural constructions, they sought to identify the *liṅga* with the king. 'Rajaraja and the Devaraja cult' has been discussed in the chapter on the Rajarajesvaram. The massive *liṅga* of unheard-of girth and height, enshrined in the most majestic temple, built by the mightiest emperor of the South, bore a direct comparison to the glory and might of the Cola monarch.

Just as the Cola monarch, Rajaraja, conquered and ruled over vast regions, the royal temple (or the royal *liṅga* in it) owned vast lands in all parts of the empire; just as the monarch commanded total allegiance and submission from his subjects, the royal temple commanded the services of people appointed from all parts of Colamandalam; just as the emperor expected tribute from the conquered provinces, the royal temple commanded the revenue of several villages from all the outlying provinces; just as the military and civil officers were under the control of the king, the royal temple had these two important sections actively involved in its affairs; just as the Cola emperor established his position as Tribhuvanacakravartin (emperor of the three worlds), the paintings and sculptures of the royal temple projected Siva as the Supreme God; just as the royal court had vast numbers of retainers, the *parivāra* of the royal temple had the largest number of functionaries; just as the court paraphernalia centred around the king, the temple paraphernalia was replete with festivals and processions mirroring the court.

In all these ways, Rajaraja adroitly duplicated the court and temple activities and substituted the *liṅga* for the royal person. Thus, when his subjects bowed in reverence to the majestic deity of Rajarajesvara, they were indirectly owing allegiance and submission to the Cola emperor. This is why the royal Cola temple had such wealth granted to it and its constituency encompassed the whole empire. This is how Rajaraja used the religious medium of the royal temple to consolidate Cola hegemony over his vast empire.

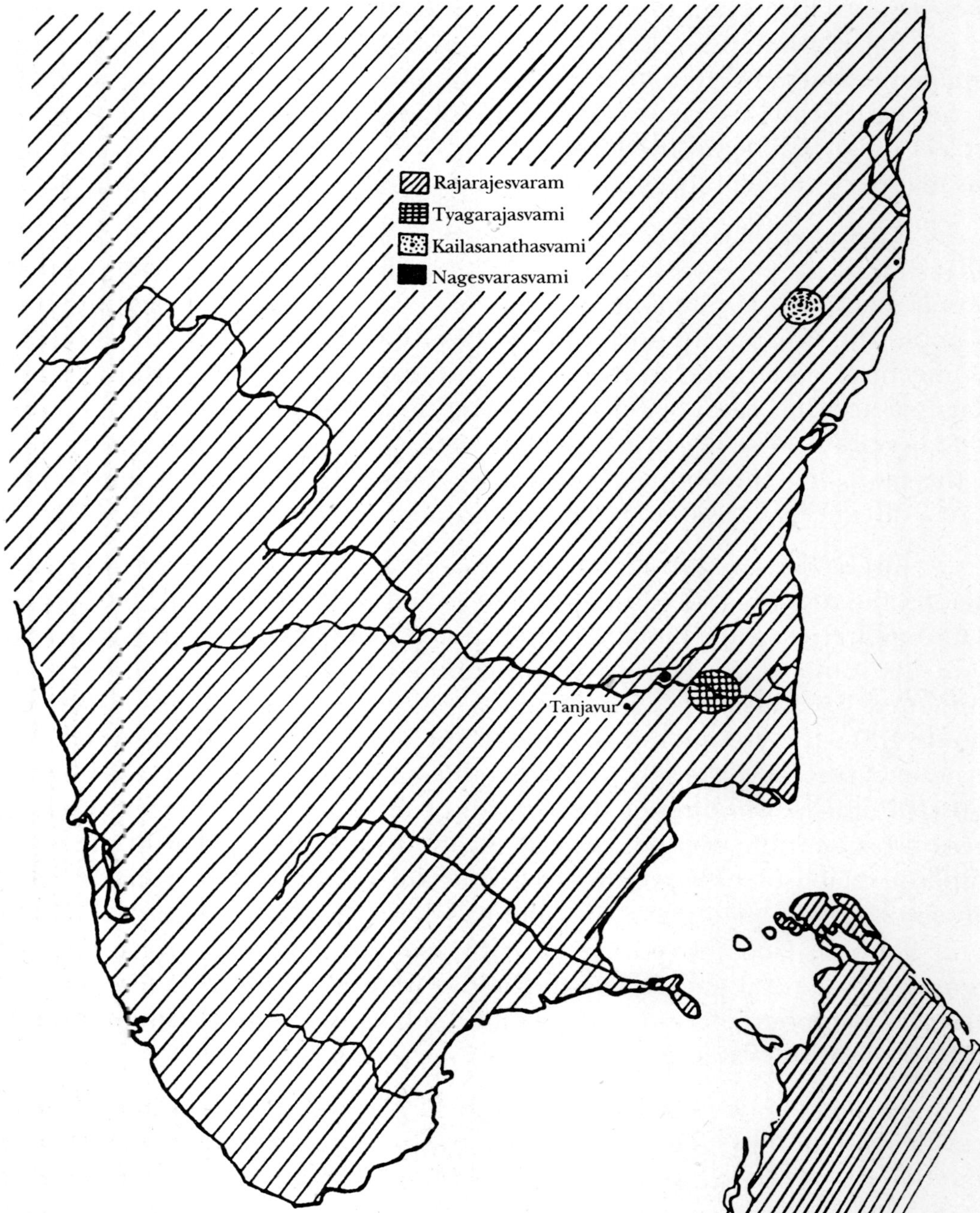

Map V: Comparative Study

BIBLIOGRAPHY

ORIGINAL SOURCES

Annual Reports on Indian Epigraphy (1887-1970).

South Indian Inscriptions, Volumes I-VIII, XII-XIV, XVII, XIX, XXI-XXIV.

Epigraphia Indica.

Epigraphia Carnatica.

Mysore Epigraphical Reports.

Tirumalai-Tirupati Epigraphical Series, Volumes I-VIII.

South Indian Temple Inscriptions, (ed.) T.N. Subramanian.

Travancore Archaeological Series.

Inscriptions of the Pudukottai State.

Thirty Pallava Copper-Plates, anon, The Tamil Varalatru Kazhagam, Madras, 1966.

A Topographical List of Inscriptions in the Tamil Nadu and Kerala States from the Earliest Times to 1300 A.D., (ed.) T.V. Mahalingam, Madras, 1919.

Museum Plates of Uttama Cola.

A Topographical List of Inscriptions of the Madras Presidency (collected till 1915), (ed.) V. Rangacharya, 3 Vols., Madras, 1919.

CHRONICLES

Koil Olugu (Chronicle of the Srirangam Temple), (ed.) V.N. Hari Rao, Madras, 1961.

Madurai Sthanikar Varalaru, Pub. in Sentamil, Volume V.

SECONDARY SOURCES

Books

Appadorai, A., Economic Conditions in Southern India (1000-1500 A.D.), Vol. I, University of Madras, 1936.

Arjun Appadurai, Worship and Conflict under Colonical Rule—A South Indian Case, Cambridge University Press, Cambridge, 1981.

Baker, C.J. and D.A. Washbrook, South India: Political Institutions and Political Changes (1880-1940), Macmillan, Delhi, 1975.

Balasubramanyam, S.R., Early Chola Art, Asia Publishing House, Bombay, 1966.

———, Early Chola Temples, Orient Longmans, New Delhi, 1971.

———, Middle Chola Temples (A.D. 985-1070), Thomson Press, 1975.

———, Later Chola Temples, Mudgala Trust, Madras, 1979.

Balasubramanyam, K., Murugan Katchi (Murugan in Tamil Literature), Madras, 1966.

Banerjea, J.N., Development of Hindu Iconography, University of Calcutta, 1956.

Basavaraja, K.R., Administration under Chalukyas of Kalyana, Madras, 1983.

Basham, A.L., The Wonder that was India, Rupa & Co., Calcutta, 1981.

Bhandarkar, R.G., Vaishnavism, Saivism and Minor Religious Systems, Varanasi, 1965.

Bhatacharya, S. & Romilla Thapar (ed.), Situating Indian History, Oxford, New Delhi, 1986.

Briggs, Lawrence P., The Ancient Khmer Empire, Philadelphia, 1951.

Chakravarti, Mahadev, The Concept of Rudra Siva Through the Ages, Delhi, 1986.

Chaterjee, B.R., Indian Cultural Influence in Cambodia, Calcutta, 1964.

Clothey, Fred. W., Images of Man: Religious and Historical Processes in South Asia, New Era, Madras, 1982.

Coward, Harold and Kawamura, L., Religion and Ethnicity, Calgary Institute, 1978.

Devakunjari, D., Madurai through the Ages—From the Earliest Times to 1801 A.D., Society for Archaeology, Madras, 1979.

Ghosh, A., The Law of Endowments, Calcutta, 1938 (2nd edn.).

Gros, R. and R. Nagaswamy, Uttaramerur: Legendes, Historie, Monuments, Pondicherry, 1970.

Gupta, K.M., The Land System in South India between 800 A.D. and 1200 A.D., Lahore, 1933.

Gururajachar, S., Economic and Social Life in Karnataka (A.D. 1000-1300), University of Mysore, 1974.

Hall, D.G.E., A History of South-East Asia, N. York, 1955.

Hall, Kenneth R., Trade and Statecraft in the Age of the Colas, Delhi, 1980.

Hari Rao, V.N., The Srirangam Temple, Tirupati, 1967.

Historicus Pseud (alias V.G. Ramakrishna Ayyar), Economy of a South Indian Temple, Pub. Ph.D. Thesis.

Ismail, I., Karnataka Temples—Their Role in Socio-Economic Life, Delhi, 1984.

Jagadeesan, N., History of Sri Vaishnavism in the Tamil Country, Madurai, 1977.

Jagadisa Ayyar, P.V., South Indian Shrines, New Delhi, 1982.

Jaisval, Suvira, The Origin and Development of Vaishnavism, Delhi, 1967.

Karashima, N., South Indian History and Society—Studies from Inscriptions A.D. 850-1800, Delhi, 1984.

———, Indus Valley to Mekong Delta, Explorations in Epigraphy, Madras, 1985.

Karashima, N., Subbarayalu, Y. & Matsui, T. (ed.), A Concordance of the Names in the Cola Inscs., Vols. I, II, Madurai, 1978.

Kosambi, D.D., An Introduction to the Study of Indian History, 2nd edn., Bombay, 1975.

———, Myth and Reality, Bombay, 1962.

Krishnan, K.G., Studies in South Indian History and Epigraphy, Madras, 1981.

Krishnaswami Aiyangar, A History of Tirupati, Vols. I & II, Madras, 1940.

______, Evolution of Hindu Administrative Institutions in South India, Madras, 1932.

Mahalingam, T.V., Administration and Social Life Under Vijayanagar, Madras, 1940.

______, Early South Indian Palaeography, University of Madras, 1969.

Minakshi, C., Administration and Social Life Under the Pallavas, Madras, 1931.

______, The Historical Sculptures of the Vaikunta Perumal Temple, Kanchi, Memoirs of ASI, 1941.

Nagaswamy, R., Gangaikondacholapuram, Madras, 1970.

______, Tanjai Peruvudaiyar Koil Kalvettugal, Dept. of Archaeology, Government of Tamil Nadu, 1969.

Nandi, R.N., Religious Institutions and Cults in the Deccan, Delhi, 1973.

Narayana Ayyar, C.V., Origin and Early History of Saivism in South India, University of Madras, 1974.

Nilakanta Sastri, K.A., The Colas, Madras, 1955.

______, The Development of Religion in South India, Madras, 1963.

______, A History of South India, 4th edn., Oxford, 1975.

Pillay, K.K., The Suchindram Temple, Madras, 1953.

Pillai, Somasundaram, J.M., The Great Temple at Tanjore, 2nd edn., Tanjore, 1958.

Ponnuswamy, S., Sri Thyagarajasvami Temple, Tiruvarur, Madras, 1972.

Rajamanickam, M., The Development of Saivism in South India Under the Pallavas of Kanchi and the Imperial Cholas, Dharmapuram Adhinam, 1964.

Raman, K.V., Sri Varadarajaswami Temple—Kanchi: A Study of its History, Art & Architecture, New Delhi, 1975.

Raman, K.V. *et al.* (ed.), Srinidhih, Perspectives in Indian Architecture, Art & Culture, Madras, 1983.

______, Some Aspects of Pandyan History, Madras, 1972.

———, The Early History of Madras Region, Madras, 1959.

Rao, Gopinatha, T.A., Elements of Hindu Iconography, 2 Vols., Delhi, 1916.

Reddy, Mooka C., The Tirumalavadi Temple—History and Culture Through the Ages, 1986.

Richard, Fox G. (ed.), Realm and Region in Traditional India, New Delhi, 1977.

Shanmugam, P., The Revenue System of the Cholas 850-1279, Madras, 1987.

Sharma, R.S., Indian Feudalism (300-1200), Calcutta, 1965.

Sarkar, H., The Kampaharesvara Temple at Tribhuvanam, Government of Tamil Nadu, Madras, 1974.

Sircar, D.C., Political and Administrative Systems of Ancient and Medieval India, Delhi, 1974.

———, Indian Epigraphy, Delhi, 1965.

Sivaramamurthi, C., The Chola Temples (3rd edn.), New Delhi, 1978.

Soundararajan, K.V., Glimpses of Indian Culture—Architecture, Art & Religion, Delhi, 1981.

Spencer, George, W., Temples, Kings and Peasants—Perceptions of South India's Past, Madras, 1987.

———, The Politics of Expansion, The Chola Conquest of Sri Lanka and Srivijaya, Madras, 1983.

Stein, Burton, Peasant State and Society in Medieval South India, Delhi, 1980.

———, All the Kings' Mana—Papers on Medieval South Indian History, Madras, 1984.

——— (ed.), Essays on South India, New Delhi, 1976.

Subba Rao, B., The Personality of India, Univ. of Baroda, 1956.

Subbarayalu, Y., Political Geography of the Chola Country, Madras, 1975.

Subramanya Aiyar, K.V., Historical Sketches of Ancient Dekhan, Vols. II & III, Coimbatore, 1969.

Sundaram, K., The Simhachalam Temple, Waltair, 1969.

Thapar, Romilla, From Lineage to State, Bombay, 1984.

Tirumalai, R., Studies in the History of Ancient Townships of Pudukkottai, Government of Tamil Nadu, Madras, 1981.

______, Land Grants and Agrarian Reactions in Cola and Pandya Times, Madras University, Archaeological Series, No. 6, 1987.

Vayiravel K. Mudaliar, Kandasasti Virada Sirappu, Sri Subramaniaswami Devasthana.

Venkatarathnam, A.V., Local Government in the Vijayanagar Empire, Univ. of Mysore, 1972.

Venkataraman, B., Rajarajesvaram: The Pinnacle of Chola Art, Madras, 1985.

Viraraghavacharya, T.K., History of Tirupati, Vols. I & II, Tirupati, 1979.

Articles

Arjun Appadurai, "Right and Left Hand Castes in South India", IESHR, XI, 1974.

______, "Kings, Sects and Temples in South India, 1350-1700 A.D.", IESHR, 1977.

Arjun Appadurai & Carol A. Breckenridge, "The South Indian Temple—Authority, Honor and Redistribution", Contributions to Indian Sociology, N.S. No. 2, 1976.

Breckenridge, Carol A., "Madurai Sthanikas: Mediators of Royal Culture", Madurai Temple Complex, Kumbhabhisheka Souvenir, 1974.

Champakalakshmi, R., "Growth of Urban Centres in South India: Kudamukku-Palaiyarai, the Twin-city of the Cholas", Studies in History, Vol. 1, 1979.

______, "Urbanisation in South India: The Role of Ideology and Polity", IHC, 1986.

______, "Religious Conflict in the Tamil Country: A Re-appraisal of Epigraphic Evidence", JESI, 1978.

______, "Ideology and the State in South India" (in press).

Dirks, Nicholas B., "Political Authority and Structural Change in Early South

Indian History", IESHR, 1976.

_______, "The Pasts of a Palaiyarar: The Ethno-History of a South Indian Little King", JAS, 1982.

Dutt, K.I., "The Historical Importance and the Economic Aspect of the South Indian Temple", Journal of the Andhra Historical Research Society, 1933.

Gough, Kathleen, "Modes of Production in Southern India", Economic & Political Weekly, 1980.

Gurukkal, Rajan, "Social Formation and Political Processes in Early Tamilakam" (in press).

Hall, Kenneth, "Peasant State and Society in Cola Times: A view from Tiruvidaimarudur Urban Complex", IESHR, 1982.

_______, "Merchants, Rulers and Priests in an Early South Indian Sacred Centre: Chidambaram in the age of the Colas", Pennsylvania, 1984.

_______, "Price-Making and Market Hierarchy in Early Medieval South India", IESHR, 1977.

Hocart, A.M., "Kings and Councillors", Comparative Anatomy of Human Society, ed. R. Needham, Chicago, 1970.

Heitzman, James, "Temple Urbanism in Medieval South India", JAS, 1987.

Jha, D.N., "Early Indian Feudalism: Historiographical Critique", IHC, 1979.

_______, "Temples and Merchants in South India (900-1300 A.D.)", Essays in Honour of Prof. S.C. Sarkar.

_______, "Relevance of Peasant State and Society to Pallava-Cola Times", Indian Historical Review, 1981-82.

Kennedy, Richard, "Status and Control of Temples in Tamil Nadu", IESHR, 1974.

Kosambi, D.D., "The Basis of Ancient Indian History", Journal of the American Oriental Society, 1955.

Krishnan, K.G., "Legacies from Rajaraja", Rajaraja the Great—Seminar, 1987.

Mahalingam, T.V., "The Nagesvarasvami Temple", JIH, 1967.

Nagaswamy, R., "South Indian Temple as an Employer", IESHR, 1965.

———, "Saivism Under Rajaraja—A Study", Rajaraja the Great—Seminar, 1987.

Nilakanta Sastri, K.A., "The Economy of a South Indian Temple in the Cola Period", Malaviya Commemoration Volume, BHU, 1932.

Pathak, V.S., "History of Saiva Cults in Northern India from Inscs. (700-1200)", Studies in History, Culture & Archaeology, 1980.

Ramachandra Dikshitar, V.R., "A Note on the Composition of Sabha at Uttaramerur", D.R. Bhandarkar Volume, Calcutta, 1940.

Raman, K.V., "Epigraphical Gleanings of Vaishnava Acharyas", Prof. K.A. Nilakanta Sastri Felicitation Volume, Madras, 1977.

———, 'Religious Trends During Rajaraja's Reign", Rajaraja the Great—Seminar, 1987.

———, "Cultural Heritage—A Synthesis", Presidential Address, IHC, 1985.

Raman, K.V. and P. Shanmugam, "Aspects of Village Settlements, Art Traditions and Village Deities in Lalgudi Taluk", Socio-Cultural Change in Villages in Trichirapalli, ed. N. Karashima, Tokyo, 1983.

Ramesh, K.V., "Cola Hegemony in South India—A Comparative & Critical Assessment, JESI, 1976.

———, "Chola Epigraphy with Special Reference to Rajaraja", Rajaraja the Great—Seminar, 1987.

Saletore, B.A., "The Sthanikas and their Historical Importance", Journal of the Univ. of Bombay, 1938.

Sanjay Subramanian, "Aspects of State Formation in South India and South East Asia, 1500-1650", IESHR, 1986.

Shanmugam, P., "Tax-free Grants During the Period of Rajaraja I, Rajaraja the Great—Seminar, 1987.

Shrimali, K.M., "Religion, Ideology and Society", IHC, Dharwad, 1988.

Sitaram, B., Noburu Karashima & Y. Subbarayalu, "A list of the Tamil Inscs. of the Cola Dynasty", Journal of Asian and African Studies, 1976.

Sivanesan, L.K., "Cidambaram Temple Administration—A Case Study", Aspects of Indian History and Culture, (ed.) C.E. Ramachandran and K.V. Raman, New Delhi, 1984.

Soundararajan, K.V., "The Kaleidoscopic Activities of Medieval Temples in the Tamilnadu", QJMS, 1952.

Spencer, George W., "Religious Networks and Royal Influence in Eleventh Century South India", Journal of Economic & Social History of the Orient, 1969.

———, "Royal Initiative Under Rajaraja I", IESHR, 1970.

———, "Heirs Apparent: Fiction and Function in Cola Mythical Genealogies", IESHR, 1984.

———, "Temple Money-lending and Livestock Redistribution in Early Tanjore", IESHR, 1968.

Srikantayya, S., "The Symbolism of the Temples", QJMS, 1921.

Srinivasan, K.R., "The Last of the Great Cola Temples", Journal of the Indian Society of Oriental Art, 1948.

Stein, Burton, "State Formation and Economy Reconsidered", Modern Asian Studies, 1985.

———, "The Segmentary State: Interim Reflections" (in press).

Subbarayalu, Y., "The Cola State and the Agrarian Order—Some Clarifications" (in press).

———, "The Peasantry of the Tiruchirapalli District from the 13th to 17th c.", Socio-Cultural Change in Villages in Tiruchirapalli Dist., (ed.) N. Karashima, Tokyo, 1983.

———, "The Cola State", Studies in History, 1982.

Tirumalai, R., "Glimpses of Cola Townships in Sri Lanka", JESI, 1982.

Vanamamalai, N., "State and Religion in the Chola Empire, Taxation for Thanjavur Temple's Music and Dance", Social Scientist, 1974.

Veluthat, Kesavan, "Royalty and Divinity: Legitimisation of Monarchical Power in South India", IHC, 1979.

______, "The Status of the Monarch: A note on the Rituals Pertaining to Kingship and their Significance in the Tamil Country", IHC, 1982.

Venkata Raghotam, "Religious Networks and the Legitimation of Power in the 14th c. South India. A study of Kumara Kampana's Politics of Intervention Arbitration", Studies in Religion and Changes, New Delhi, 1983.

______, "Rajendra Chola's Raid on Srivijaya in A.D. 1025", Tamil Civilization, Tamil Univ., Tanjavur, 1983.

Unpublished Theses

Chandrakumar, T., Vriddhagirisvara Temple—Vriddhachalam, Madras Univ., 1983.

Choudary, Kiran Kranth D., Srikalahastisvara Temple—Srikalahasti, Srivenkatesvara Univ., Tirupati, 1988.

Desayar, M., Temple Adminstration Under the Pandyas, Madurai, Kamaraj Univ., 1987.

Dourga, R., Temple, Cult and Politics in Early Medieval South India: An Epigraphical Study of Vakur, M.Phil. Diss., Pondicherry Univ., 1989.

Hari Rao, V.N., A History of Trichinopoly and Srirangam, Madras University, 1948.

Mira Devi, T.S., Temple Administration and Culture Under the Later Pandyas: A Case Study of the Temples of Tenkasi, Madurai, Kamaraj University, 1984.

Palanichamy, N., Brahampurisvara Temple at Trisulam, Madras University, 1979.

Ramasamy R., The Saptarisivara Temple at Lalgudi, Madras University, 1982.

Sivaprakasam, C.K., Saiva Mathas in the Tamil Country—A Historical Study, Madras University, 1985.

Subramaniam, A., Religious Endowments in the Tamil Country—A Study, Madras University, 1976.

Thilagavathi, A., Tiruvennainallur Temples, Madras University, 1989.

Varadarajan, P., Growth of Religious Institutions Under the Cholas, Madras University, 1987.

Vasantha Bai, T.R., History of Thanjavur Through the Ages, Madras University, 1976.

Vasudevan, Geeta, A Study of the Temple Administration and Temple Functionaries in Selected Temples of the Tamil Country in the Ancient Period, M.Phil. Diss., Madras University, 1984.

INDEX